Entrepreneurial Spirits

Troy D White

Spirituality, Science and Success...

Unlocking The Simple Path To Living Your Dream Life

I am on a voyage of discovery. I search for those of you who will go on a great adventure . . . if you are one of those audacious few willing to dare and then to share... then come with me. ~ William H. Danforth, **I Dare You! (1931)**

"The thing always happens that you really believe in; and the belief in a thing makes it happen." --Frank Lloyd Wright

"If you want to conquer fear, don't sit at home and think about it. Go out and get busy. " --Dale Carnegie

For information, email troy@entrepreneurialspirits.com

Printed in Canada, First Edition. ISBN 0-9736784-3-7

LEGAL NOTICE: This publication is designed to provide competent and reliable information regarding the subject matters covered. However, it is sold with the understanding that the authors and publisher are not engaged in rendering any legal, financial, or other professional advice whatsoever.

Laws and practices do vary from country to country and should legal or other specialist assistance be required, the services of a competent and suitably qualified professional should be sought.

All companies and people mentioned or profiled were selected by the author solely for the purposes of illustration. All are successful and reputable companies, to the author's best knowledge, but in no case should the inclusion of any company in this book be interpreted as an endorsement or recommendation by the author. No guarantees of similar income are made. The author and publisher specifically disclaim any liability, loss, risk, personal or otherwise which is incurred as a consequence, directly or indirectly, from the use or application of any of the contents of this book.

All trademarks, product names and company names or logos cited or used in the book are the property of their respective owners. While all attempts to verify the information provided have been taken, the author assumes no responsibility for errors, omissions, or contrary interpretation of the subject matter herein.

Any perceived slights of companies, products, organizations or peoples are unintentional. The purchaser or reader assumes all

Cover photo by Jon Sullivan: http://pdphoto.org/index.php

Visit our web site at:
http://www.entrepreneurialspirits.com/

The Guide to Entrepreneurial Spirits

Introduction

When I finally "got it", I was dumbfounded. Spirituality and success, to me, were worlds apart – until that fruitful day when I clued in.

On a private conference call, a man I highly respected told those on the call that he was VERY spiritual – yet did not talk about it at all. His closest friends knew, but that was about it. His spiritual beliefs and practices were used *every* day to create wealth beyond most people's imagination and were used to help tens of thousands of people across the world lead better, happier, and more profitable lives.

It dawned on me right then and there.

If he is highly spiritual and doesn't talk about it – are most highly successful people spiritual as well?

The findings I uncovered amazed me… up to 75% of the highly successful people I spoke with - and surveyed – WERE spiritual people as well. Yet few of them talked about it outside of their close circle.

Ah, I smell a subject with some controversy! Something so critically important to those desiring success – yet few want to talk about one of the inner circle secrets! So, I wanted to break the code and get people's thoughts.

And it took on a life of its own. As you will soon see – success and spirituality DO go hand in hand. In fact it is one of the requirements of business with the 57 people in this book.

The advice here is priceless – if you apply it.

"There is no use whatever trying to help people who do not help themselves. You cannot push anyone up a ladder unless he be willing to climb himself." -- Andrew Carnegie

Unlimited success, peace, happiness and prosperity are yours with the tools and advice in this book.

Please use them – the authors in this book wanted you to have this gift of knowledge. It is up to you to apply the knowledge and create the success and happiness in your life that you desire.

You will notice a difference in the type of replies within – exactly what I had hoped for.

Some of the authors answered the questions I asked them, some decided to tell a story, and some created books in themselves for this anthology. What amazed me, as I'm sure it will you, is the breadth of wisdom these people contributed.

Enjoy and prosper with the advice you discover within.

Troy White
Entrepreneurial Spirits
403.259.4566
troy@entrepreneurialspirits.com

PS – I was also very fortunate to be part of a group called Entrepreneurial Spirits (I loved the name so much… I bought the company… ok more like borrowed the name for this book).

The original Entrepreneurial Spirits was headed up by a fantastic gal, Jeanne Cummings. She is travelling right now in Thailand and unfortunately could not take part in this book. Rest assured though – you will hear a lot more about her successes in the future.

In 1948, in his book, "The Magic of Believing," Claude M. Bristol said:

"I am cognizant of the fact that there are powerful forces at work in this country that would dominate us, substituting a kind of regimentation for the competitive system which has made America great among nations. They would attempt to destroy individual thinking and initiative, cherished ever since our Pilgrim Fathers established this country in defiance of the Old World tyranny.

I believe that we must continue to retain the wealth of spirit of our forefathers, for if we don't we shall find ourselves dominated in everything we do by a mighty few and shall become serfs in fact if not in name."

"Reduce your plan to writing... The moment you complete this, you will have definitely given concrete form to the intangible desire." - Napoleon Hill

---

John Assaraf

1) New information reveals that 75%+ of the world's most successful people are profoundly spiritual in both belief and practice. Describe how your personal and business success has evolved through Spiritual Influences.

For many years now I have been paying attention to the perfection that exists in me and all around me. I have taken the stance that we live in a highly intelligent universe and that our creator is ever present in everything at all time.

In knowing this, I believe that every moment is divine perfection without fail. I do not confuse things or circumstances that are not to my taste in my personal and professional life, and say that they are "bad" or "wrong."

There cannot be that distinction in a divine and orderly universe. When asked "where is GOD not?" I feel that as long as I realize the perfection in all things at all times I am in flow with divinity.

Any success I have achieved is due to the integration of my beliefs about GOD with my behaviour.

The more I believe, the more I succeed.

2) In what ways do you incorporate your Spiritual Beliefs into day-to-day business interactions?

I trust that everything happens for a reason that serves me even though I may not see it at the time. I ask GOD for guidance and trust the response implicitly.

3) What is the single-most important spiritual practice that promotes peace and prosperity within your own life?

The two most important spiritual practices for me are love and gratitude.

4) Imagine you are having a conversation with God (or the Universal creator or whatever name you prefer)... Share with us what is being said about the scope and future of Spirituality in the Entrepreneurial Business world.

What is being said by God is "those who shall see me and take me into their heart and mind, will bring about the joys of creation."

* * * * * * * *

John Assaraf
New York Times @ Wall Street Journal Bestselling Author, Speaker, Entrepreneur
http://www.thestreetkid.com
Phone: (858) 759-9527
Fax: (858) 777-5740
email:john@thestreetkid.com

"That which you think today becomes which you are tomorrow. " - Napoleon Hill

---

Rick Beneteau

1) New information reveals that 75%+ of the world's most successful people are profoundly spiritual in both belief and practice. Describe how your personal and business success has evolved through Spiritual Influences.

I was fortunate to have been both an energetic entrepreneur and a "positive thinker" from early on in my adult life. Coupled with my passion for music, traits I inherited from my late, great father.

Running a drycleaning business and a songwriting enterprise in my twenties, I was also fortunate to have absorbed the amazing wisdom contained in books by Bob Proctor (who now represents my products), Wallace D. Wattles, Napolean Hill and others.

Couple this early discovery of the "truths of the Universe" with what has always been a built-in desire to help people, in business and otherwise, well, I guess you could say I had all the necessary ingredients in order to conduct whatever business I've had (and there have been plenty) on a spiritual level.

With that said, I think the horrific events of September 11, 2001, had millions of people on this planet turn inwards to discover their true spirituality and that is now being reflected in how people approach operating their businesses.

In fact, this tragedy inspired me to completely change my direction on the Internet from that of helping people to build their online businesses to just trying to help build people.

My first two projects reflect that change. My private site, People Building People (http://www.peoplebuildingpeople.com), and then the blockbuster eBook, Success: A Spiritual Matter (http://www.onlygoodbusiness.com) are about applying simple spiritual **values to enhance your personal and business life as well as positively impact people all around you.**

My prediction is that in spite of the suffering and chaos in the world (started and maintained by the 'unspiritual', of course), this trend towards a kinder, more spiritual business world will continue to grow. A good thing.

2) In what ways do you incorporate your Spiritual Beliefs into day-to-day business interactions?

First, let me say that I believe there is NO distinction between living a spiritual personal life and a spiritual business life. They are inseparable and I witness this reality in the lives of the many amazing "Entrepreneurial Spirits" I am blessed to have come to know.

Practically speaking though, and in order for me to answer your question Troy, let me outline some of the things I incorporate, and try to improve on, as I go through the daily grind of doing business.

As my yardstick, I try to live by the Universal Law of Attraction i.e.: "what you think about, what you visualize, you attract into your life" simply because I **know** that everything I "put out there" will come back to me in kind. Positive thoughts and positive practices produce positive results.

In fact, my latest product (http://www.bettersalesrightnow.com) is all about thinking "success thoughts", the same kinds of thoughts that the most successful entrepreneurs in the world think that are totally responsible for the great success they have achieved.

I can tell you in all certainty that those times when a product or business of mine wasn't successful or even failed, that I was **not** thinking the kinds of thoughts that would have created the opposite result. The most powerful force on the planet is **your thinking**!

I also try very hard to exercise the virtue of patience, not so easy to do when you are a taskmaster Virgo, with my affiliates, with my customers, with my subscribers and with my business partners. In all situations.

For instance, I sell digital products. With email the way it is these days - with spam, spam filters, personal email filters, email just doesn't get through like it did in 1998 when I first logged on. So, say a customer did not receive their order confirmation email, containing the download links, because their ISP blocked it. There was a time when I would receive that snarly, angry customer email a few hours later stating that they had been ripped off and I was a thief and blah, blah in the most offensive language imaginable, that I would get a little belligerent in return and fire off an emotionally charged email in response. After all, it was MY integrity they were attacking!

Today, I simply "kill all such people with kindness", and in this case I would simply explain that we were sorry they didn't receive their downloads instantaneously and then gently provide what they had purchased. The world needs SO much more kindness and patience these 'daze'.

Many of my quotes from articles and things I have written are now featured in popular ezines on the internet and one that expresses "over-delivery" of a product or service to a customer, a core belief of mine, is this: "Sell a Meg, Give a Gig!" What the heck, here's another (I love quotes:-): "Sell a customer what they want, deliver what they need."

Point here is that more than ever, when I am developing a new product, I begin with a product template that is "over-delivery" to begin with and from there I start building on that so as to benefit my customer 'squared'.

Above all, learn this one immense but simple secret for success. We all have challenges and face problems. Often, they are serious and seem insurmountable. Your solution: Be Still, allow the answers to flow to you. The Universe contains every solution you will ever need. Simply offer up your request, and let it go. Your solution **will** appear. Like magic. It is in 'the silence' that the solutions lie.

Troy, I may risk being the most long-winded of your contributors, however, I want to offer your readers what are my core beliefs here in a "chart" I wrote called:

The Seller's Creed

I will not make sales. I will make Customers.

I will target the heart of my Customer. Never their wallet.

My Customer is the lifeblood of my business.

Though I may sell my Customers what they want,
I will deliver what they need and make their lives better.

Courtesy and Service are cornerstones of my relationship with my Customer.

I will view complaints as opportunities . . .opportunities to create lifelong Customers.

The quality of my products and how I treat my Customers will determine the level of My Success.

My prosperity will come from 'growing' people.

My best advertisement is my product and the Customer service behind it.

Making money without making friends is not good business.

I will guide my business with the perfect blend of heart and mind.

I will make Integrity my trademark. After all, isn't integrity all I have and all I will be remembered for?

I will compete only against myself as the only true measurement is against myself.

It is fine to fail. In fact, it is most often a requirement of success.

My reputation is everything - my ego, nothing.
Every pittance I earn unjustly is a debt of fortune I must repay.

No matter the fame or fortune that may follow me,
My values, My family and My friends must remain at the very core of my being.

Better I be trusted and respected, than be materially rich.

Better I be a dolphin swimming with sharks, than a shark.

© 2001 Rick Beneteau

If you want to hear me recite this with music that I wrote for my father playing in the background, please visit: http://www.bettersalesrightnow.com/creed.mp3

3) What is the single-most important spiritual practice that promotes peace and prosperity within your own life?

"Just be your true, spiritual self." I really mean that. Bring your spirituality to both your personal AND business life, and you will succeed. No doubt about it. Treat others as you would treat yourself, and even better, and you are well on your way to success in all areas of your life. I absolutely guarantee it! My only short answer☺

4) Imagine you are having a conversation with God (or the Universal creator or whatever name you prefer)… Share with us what is being said about the scope and future of Spirituality in the Entrepreneurial Business world.

Troy, please allow me to twist this question around for the benefit of your readers, and express to your readers what **I** have asked of the Universe by sharing my "Entrepreneur's Prayer", with apologies to those who may have come across it before:

The Entrepreneur's Prayer

As I awaken with the gift of yet another day and prepare for the tasks at hand, I offer up this most ardent prayer:

I pray for continued clarity of purpose so that I may hold my vision steady and keep my focus on the needs and success of others, which in turn shall bring me my success.

I pray for the wisdom to expect abundance in my life, that it surrounds me and is available for the taking and to be shameless and unapologetic upon its receipt, for I deserve abundance.

I pray for a cheerful countenance, be it clear or cloudy skies and that I may radiate and infect others with my positive attitude.

I pray for the trust of others that they may recognize my sincerity and true intentions so that we may move forward together.

I pray for the strength to fend off adversity and use my desire and determination as both weapon and shield.

I pray for the courage to carry forth my convictions during the battle of business and to resist temptation to a quicker monetary result when such temptation compromises these things for which I stand.

I pray that I may be used as a lightning rod to collect the amazing ideas already present in the universe and when blessed with such inspiration, that I may be able to apply my talents and abilities to turn the power of thought into measurable advancement of my goals.

I pray to retain my childhood wonder so that I can recognize and revel in the small miracles of each day that others may miss.

I pray for an infinite supply of self-confidence for it alone fortifies faith, strengthens my resolve and conquers the largest enemy I will ever face - fear.

I pray for a compassionate spirit and the patience to offer those who seek my advice and my help, my full and undivided attention.

I pray for good health and a feeling of well being, and the continued desire to improve those areas of my physical life I may be neglecting in the name of my spiritual and entrepreneurial advancement.

I pray that today is a day of excellence and at its conclusion I can acknowledge and be grateful for the forward motion I have made and the growth I have experienced.

I pray most of all for the understanding and support of those closest to my heart, my family, that they will equate what may seem like endless hours of apparent pre-occupation with affairs of business to what is at the very core of my being, that which drives me, for once I achieve what I have set out in its fullest, I will become that more complete being I strive to be.

It is for these things that I pray, for I am an entrepreneur.

© 1998 Rick Beneteau

If you want to hear my great friend, former music and now Internet partner, Larry Thompson, recite this with music that he wrote playing in the background, please visit:
http://www.bettersalesrightnow.com/prayer.mp3

And if would like a beautiful 11" x 14" print of The Entrepreneur's Prayer, please visit:
http://www.rickbeneteau.com/prints/index.htm

3) What is the best piece of advice you could offer readers of "Entrepreneurial Spirits" right here, and right now?"

Trust the Universe. It is biased towards 'good'. Don't allow the overshadowing evil in the world to dissuade you from moving forward with your spiritual values and growth. Bring ALL that you are, and truly believe in, and wholeheartedly represent, to your business and personal life.

If everyone did this, think of what our world would be like!

Troy, thank you very much for the honor of doing this interview. My sincere hope is that your readers will benefit from something I've said. I wish to leave your readers with a gift. It is a song I wrote over a decade ago that was recently resurrected as a bonus for one of my new products.

It's called "Forgiveness" and I hope you enjoy it:
:http://peoplebuildingpeople.com/files/forgiveness.mp3

* * * * * * * *

Rick Beneteau

Award winning author Rick Beneteau is the co-creator of the blockbuster eBook that Joe Vitale calls "Astonishing. Unforgettable. Electrifying... It's a masterpiece!",

Success: A Spiritual Matter is available at:
http://www.onlygoodbusiness.com.

Rick invites you to subscribe to his ARISE! Ezine
(http://www.arise.themirrorezine.com)
and also to **Make Every Day A Great Day.**

"It's kind of fun to do the impossible." -- Walt Disney

Kim Buck

1. Describe how my personal and business success has evolved through Spiritual practices.

My personal success and business success have evolved through two main concepts. The first is trust. I had to learn to trust that there was a force inside me, and outside me, that was much greater than I was working with me at all times. This meant that there was a natural rhythm and timing to everything, including my readiness to take the next step, whatever that was. It also meant that lots of things were beyond my control and that I had to stop trying to control things I had no control over. I also had to learn that trust is an action and it is the most significant and most difficult action to take; to sit back and trust that this force, the Universe, was doing what needed to be done without me stepping in and messing things up.

Most people believe taking action is actually physically doing something that results in things moving along and that sitting back and trusting is something that unmotivated, uncommitted and unproductive people do that produces no results. In fact, it is just the opposite. My current work came to me when I finally stopped trying to create or think of what I should be doing with my life and instead sat back, trusted that it would be presented to me and allowed it to be. If I tried to get involved and busy myself with "doing something productive" I'd still be miserable doing what I didn't enjoy doing, all the while wondering what my true purpose was.

My success has also evolved through the conscious reconnection with my feminine energy. For a long time, the feminine aspect of myself was shut down. This is very common with women today because feminine energy has been so disrespected and unappreciated for so long and only the masculine aspects of ourselves have been rewarded and honored. I was totally out of balance with who I was. Having worked around masculine energy day in and day out, I was craving the balance of feminine energy. I also understood on some level that it is the feminine aspect of us that connects to our higher self that allows us to create great things.

I made a conscious decision to reconnect with my feminine energy and it was through this reconnection that my current work has evolved. It is through this feminine energy that I am helping others heal, have compassion for others, want the best for others and help others be or become all that they can be.

2. In what ways do I incorporate my Spiritual beliefs into day-to-day business interaction?

I know that I benefit when others are happy and successful so I do what I can to help others become happy and successful. Furthermore, I hire or work only with those who want me to succeed. I eliminate contact with anyone who does not want me to succeed or is not interested in my success. This way, I keep my energy high which enables me to do what I need to do and to help others do what they need to do.

I always want what is in my greatest good and the good of all concerned and when interacting with others I always quietly ask that the interaction be in our greatest and highest good. I attract clients who want what I offer and I work with people who offer what I need. I do not expect others to change their business model for me and I do not change my business model for people that I cannot serve.

I seek my truth in all interactions and I connect with those who are also seeking their truth. My most powerful interactions are with those who also speak their truth and know their truth. If I meet someone who is not willing to speak their truth, I know that we will not be on the same wavelength and the interaction or relationship will not be a good fit.

In all interactions, I trust my intuition.

I seek to inspire everyone I meet. Everyone can be inspired about who they are and what they offer the world. To me, inspiring others about themselves is where the music is.

I realize that everyone is where they are at and I don't know what has gone on for them before we met. So, I don't make assumptions about where they should be and what they should want. I also don't make assumptions about what others may be thinking of me because I have no way of knowing for sure. And, I don't take people's comments personally because I know that it is not about me. If people could just learn this and live by it, the world would be a much better place – don't take it personally, it is NOT about you.

3. What is the single most important spiritual practice that promotes peace and prosperity within my own life?

For me, the single most important spiritual practice is my daily journaling. It is through journaling that I connect with my inner wisdom, my higher self. I started journaling daily about 3 years ago when I had no sense of direction and I hated the work that I was doing. I started out by asking the question, "What makes my heart sing?" By answering this question every day for several weeks, the work I am supposed to be doing and am doing started to appear on the paper. By asking this question over and over, and by being willing to discover the answers, the voice within me started to speak. This led me to the work I do today. I went from not having a clue about my purpose and what I should be doing with my life to the work I am doing now, which I love.

I continue to journal daily and I use it to ask the questions I want answers to. The answers always come out, maybe not immediately and not always on the page, but I always receive the answers. When I ask the questions, I always write that I choose to hear the words of my higher self and the Universe. The more I ask, the more answers I receive. I also use my daily journaling to express gratitude for everything and everyone I have in my life. And, when I express gratitude for those really close to my heart, I find myself filled with an enormous sense of receiving from the world. Expressing gratitude is one of the best ways I have found to elevate my day.

4. Share what is being said about the scope and future of Spirituality in the entrepreneurial business world.

Spirituality must be and is becoming an accepted part of the business world. We can no longer run businesses that are devoid of spiritual principles. We see this now. Businesses that in the past were run solely for profit and greed are crumbling. Businesses that take advantage of others or offer empty promises, products or services are falling apart. We are no longer willing to be okay with that type of company. People are awakening and the mass consciousness is rising in vibration. We are now part of the inspiration economy and people crave to be inspired by their leaders and by the companies they work for. We are no longer simply satisfied with a paycheck and life-long employment. We now want to feel fulfilled. We want to feel like our contribution meant something and that it was part of our master plan, not simply an avenue to an end for the company. This is shifting both what work is done and the way work is done.

Three significant shifts that are already in play in the business world are: 1) the increased focus on the Divine Feminine principle; 2) the shift in focus from outcome to process and 3) how success and shareholder value are determined.

The increased focus on the Divine Feminine principle is a substantial shift away from the wholly exclusive focus on the masculine principle. More and more people are asking what their purpose is and they are not content to do work that does not honor that purpose. Work is no longer just about making money or accumulating market share. It is now more about being creative, and providing products and services that enhance people's sense of who they are and what they offer the world. Work is becoming more about helping others, healing others, enlightening others. The proliferation of services such as healing practices and coaching is evidence to this.

As we move away from operating strictly under the masculine approach to business, we find the focus is also shifting from outcome to process. The focus-on-outcome model for doing business essentially says that we will reach our target at all costs. The focus-on-process model means that we ask questions such as, "Are we doing the right thing?" "Are we inspiring everyone on the team to be their best?" "Are we providing services that benefit others; that help others achieve what they want to achieve?" "Are we honoring our people's needs for balance outside of work?" This will be a difficult transition for those whose sole focus has been on achieving goals and targets. It will seem like little is being accomplished when the focus is on process. However, when we focus on the process, the outcome will be guaranteed. When we focus only on the outcome, sooner or later we will fall because we haven't taken into account the human price of "outcome at all costs."

As we continue to move into the energy of the Divine Feminine principle, success will be based not on how much money the company made but on how well all people connected to the company, the employees, vendors, and clients/customers are treated. Shareholder value will be derived through the level of abundance created for all individuals connected to the company. The greater the wealth created for each and every person connected to a company, the more attractive the company will be to shareholders and the higher the shareholder value. This is such a departure from how shareholder value is determined right now.

* * * * * * * *

Kim Buck
Helping people release their pain, release their weight and empower themselves.
What Have You Got to Lose!
http://www.whathaveyougottolose.ca
info@whathaveyougottolose.ca
403-701-1525

The best and most beautiful things in this world cannot be seen or even heard, but must be felt with the heart. - Helen Keller

---

Bob Burg

1) New information reveals that 75%+ of the world's most successful people are profoundly spiritual in both belief and practice. Describe how your personal and business success has evolved through Spiritual Influences.

I believe that, in the same way that G-d is One, that everything we are and everything we do is also one thing. In other words, whether personal or business, we are the same person, and that business life and personal life while they can be separate as far as actual activity can not be separate regarding the essence of a person - their soul, their spirituality.

For example, I've often heard people say they are one way at work and another at home. In other words, they take pride in that they are ruthless at work but kind at home. Or, they are dishonest in their work life but honest in their personal life. I don't believe that is so. The essence of a person manifests both in the business and in the personal aspects of their life.

So, how do you run your personal life/business life? Through what belief system do you operate your personal life/business life? Micah 6:8 says, "and what does the L-rd require of you? Only to do justly, love kindness/mercy and walk humbly with G-d." Is this always on the forefront of your mind when dealing with prospects, clients, suppliers and co-workers? What about your loved ones? Or, the toll-booth collector, waitperson at the restaurant and person behind you in line at the supermarket?

My spiritual focusing puts G-d as the General Manager of the Universe. This helps me both in my personal and business lives because I can relax and know that so long as I do my best, G-d will take care of the rest.

Once I figured that out (though, please believe me, I need to keep working on it; I often find myself having to re-learn this) it took a lot of the pressure off of me. I came to the realization that the only thing I could control was my own activity, my own actions, and that that was enough. It allowed me to realize that I could (as Wallace D. Wattles wrote in his excellent 1910 book, The Science of Getting Rich) live on the creative plane instead of the competitive plane.

This attitude allows one to focus on doing their best, and having oneself as ones only competition. Comparisons are only with oneself, and the only measurement is how did I do today as opposed to yesterday or the day before?

2) What is the single-most important spiritual practice that promotes peace and prosperity within your own life?

Doing my very best in trying to serve my market. There is a very strong correlation between the principle of Free Enterprise and spirituality.

For example, in a free enterprise-based economy, the amount of money you make is directly proportional to how many people you serve. Isn't that also a wonderful spiritual principle? You are actually rewarded based on how many people you serve and how much value you bring to the marketplace. We can take the above saying even further by saying, if you want to make a lot of money, then find a lot of people to serve and serve them well.

How does this bring me peace and prosperity? Because I know that if I can focus on serving others, I'll feel good about myself and bring in enough money to live a comfortable lifestyle. Combine that with doing something you love and believe in (also a very spiritual principle) and you have a life of true joy and serenity. WOW!

3) Imagine you are having a conversation with God (or the Universal creator or whatever name you prefer)- Share with us what is being said about the scope and future of Spirituality in the Entrepreneurial Business world.

I believe that such a conversation would direct me to do my best to promote spirituality to the business world. This relates to the first thing we discussed in this questionnaire; that since G-d is One and everything else is one, that spirituality in the entrepreneurial business world is good for everyone involved.

* * * * * * * *

Bob Burg (http://www.burg.com) is an internationally known author and speaker on the topics of Business Networking, Positive Persuasion, and Success Principles. Among his books are Endless Referrals, Winning Without Intimidation and The Success Formula.

"As long as one keeps searching, the answers come." -- Joan

Jennifer Burgess

Spirituality and Business...
Are they separate or the same?
Without one will the other survive?

It has been proven time and time again by the most highly successful people in the world that spiritual principals (Laws of the Universe) have assisted personal, business, relationship and financial growth that would never have been possible with the human mind alone.

Just imagine a life of success, joy, love and abundance without struggle. I already know that by reading this book, these are things you want in life. Realize that by wanting or desiring more for yourself that you are not creating anything new. All you desire is already out there - ask in the right way and you shall receive.

First of all, you need to understand what the word 'Spirituality' means to you. If you don't already know then before you read any further, please take the next thirty seconds to close your eyes and discover how 'being spiritual' assists you in your daily life.

As a Clinical Hypnotherapists, we help transform lives everyday and we know that words have a different meaning to each person based on personal conditioning. Eighty percent of these conditioned belief systems are formed in our early childhood years. Parents, teachers, religion, society, government, advertising and so on... all tell us what we should and shouldn't do. They tell us to be like everyone else and that making mistakes is bad. They say don't do anything that wouldn't be accepted by the masses and of course the old, 'be seen and not heard' phrase. Do any of these, sound familiar to you?

Understand that it is our image that creates our reality. To discover what your image is, take a close look around you and you will know exactly what your conditioned mind is creating for you. Are you completely happy with your life right now? If the answer is no, then you must learn how to change internally before you can see the results you want in your reality. The way we see and judge events in our life is not always the true meaning or intention they were derived from because we are only looking at the situation from one perspective - ours. Which means that each person's reality is different, there is no right or wrong, no good or bad, just perception. Our reality is also based on how we feel at any given time, which can be different from one moment to the next.

For many, spirituality is being connected to the essence of life and becoming more aware of what we are capable of and who we actually are – Superconscious Spirit, all knowing, all loving, all encompassing. Spirit doesn't judge nor criticize, instead It loves unconditionally, wholeheartedly and is always there to support us on whatever path we may choose. Spirit has the answers, solutions and resolutions to all situations and problems in our life, no matter what's going on. No matter where you are in life, there will always be problems however, these same problems that where once mountains may now appear as small rolling hills.

In my profession, I am able to connect with the energy and essence of my clients to have a profound level of understanding of the underlying issue and how to work through it. Subsequently, I am able to help more people feel better about themselves and live a life of happiness and abundance. It is truly an honor each and everyday to be able to watch people change right in front of my eyes and make a lot of money while doing what I love. I am able to look at every situation and person from a place of love. If we could just treat everyone (including ourselves) as if they are already expressing their true potential, we would be a much more advanced and successful civilization. I challenge you to try this for one week with everyone you meet. Within seven days from today, please send me an email with how your personal and business life has improved – I guarantee it will!

I wish I could tell you there is only one thing that equals success but in fact it is a combination of several elements that attributes to highly successful people.

Take 100% responsibility for your life. Doing this means that you can change whatever you don't want and enhance what you are already good at. Try it! For one week take complete responsibility for your entire life. No more complaining, blaming or denying.

Keep an open and optimistic mind. We have two minds – the human and the Spirit. It is very easy to know which mind you are coming from because anything negative that is filled with doubt, lack and limitation is that of the human mind or otherwise known as the negative ego. While anything positive, loving and supportive is coming from the Spirit mind. When you know your thoughts are coming from the human mind, simply say "thank you for sharing". This is a good technique for quieting the mind and detaching from negativity. When coming from Spirit, you will be very productive and efficient and enjoy each step of the way. Live life based in joy and purpose vs. fear and obligation. Ask yourself; does this choice bring me closer to my purpose in life? Take time to rest. People who push themselves too hard to succeed, usually end up burning out quickly. Make time each week to stay away from your business and enjoy the day without any stress. When you return to work you will be more focused, productive and creative.

Remember everyday to be grateful for what you have and thankful for all the little miracles you experience each day.

I dare you to actually apply these basic spiritual principals today and encourage you to share with me your results via email. I look forward to reading all about your new found successes.

If you don't believe you are living up to your true potential in your business, financial or personal life, contact me today for a free fifteen-minute phone consultation.

Also, with the purchase of this book, receive 15% off the tuition to begin your career in Hypnotherapy today.

* * * * * * * *

Jennifer Burgess, M.H. C.Ht., PhD (Candidate)
Clinical Hypnotherapist
Full Circle Hypnosis
Calgary, Alberta, Canada
Email: fullcirclehypnosis@shaw.ca
Web: http://www.fullcirclehypnosis.com

"Wealth is the product of man's capacity to think."--Ayn Rand

---

Shirley Burroughs

How my personal and business success has evolved through Spiritual influences…

Going back to the beginning; I remember vividly – looking at my life and saying to myself, "I am in a state of despair but I know there is a better way to live my life. Please show me!" Almost immediately I was lead to information and people who offered me spiritual knowledge, which rang true in the very core of my being.

I became aware that I was the keeper of the keys to my life. I was to step forward, take the keys of Spirit and unlock the doors held tight by years of feeling mainly lack and unworthiness. I opened one of the doors and became aware that I had all the tools (answers) inside of myself to build a life that would shine and sparkle with success.

There was a power and wisdom I possessed that would show me the way.

Opening another door prompted me to look deeply at myself-personally. I found characteristics that I knew were valuable. I had a lot of love in my heart. But unfortunately it was mostly all devoted to others. I had forgotten to love myself. I also had a love for singing happy songs.

Children inspired me- I loved their simplicity and enthusiasm. A voice within me was saying, "These are some of your talents and abilities. They are the things you enjoy doing, build on these abilities, they are your gifts, expand them."

So I stepped forward using the power, talents and abilities I already had, but did not recognize.

This has lead me to another door and into another place, where I am writing three children's books and making three CD's which will contain ten little children's songs, that I have written. I am realizing more and more success by being aware of the Spirit within. My personal life holds much joy! This is an on going or evolving process that I am thrilled to take part in, even though I am a grandmother.

It's never too late to shine!

In what ways do you incorporate your spiritual beliefs into day-to- day business interactions?

I see the power and potential in myself and others. This brings forward the best into my business and my world.

The single most important spiritual practice that promotes peace and prosperity within my life is BEING who I am, in Truth. For example: being creative, being positive, being love, being happy, being understanding, being confident, while releasing all the negative nay-sayers, both from within myself and from without.

They are the bandits that hold us back.

I had a conversation with Spirit in which I asked what is being said about the scope and future of Spirituality in the Entrepreneurial Business world.

The answer will be the realization that Spiritual wisdom and power exists in all situations in life. Answers and solutions are forthcoming when a person in business makes a firm choice and then knows and accepts, without a doubt, that this choice will be realized. There is a second part to this answer and it is the fact that the entrepreneurial business world of the future must hold firm to RIGHT CONDUCT in all of their affairs. Following the path of Spiritual Righteousness will assure success for all. We will create dominion rather than domination.

"Follow your instincts. That's where true wisdom manifests itself."
-- Oprah Winfrey

Dr. Carolle

1) New information reveals that 75%+ of the world's most successful people are profoundly spiritual in both belief and practice. Describe how your personal and business success has evolved through Spiritual Influences.

As a physician who has worked with patients from the poorest women of Haiti to the wealthiest of Southern California, I've found that there are four key components of health, which together determine the overall well-being and quality of your life: mental, physical, spiritual, and financial aspects. But each aspect can contribute to stress and physical problems. Just like a four-legged table, if just one is off kilter, the table will wobble, or topple over.

The majority of patients during midlife who are experiencing negative emotional symptoms such as fear, anxiety, panic attacks depression, and worry do not have a strong spiritual base in their lives. The spiritual leg of the table is one of the strongest.

2) In what ways do you incorporate your Spiritual Beliefs into day-to-day business interactions?

I am a board-certified gynaecologist, a medical intuitive for midlife women issues......Part of our health questionnaire includes a spiritual history. Most health plans given to my patients include suggestions on how to improve or forge a stronger spiritual bond with their higher power.

3) What is the single-most important spiritual practice that promotes peace and prosperity within your own life?

Learning to surrender and having faith that all is well and that I will be taken care of, no matter what.

4) Imagine you are have a conversation with God (or the Universal Creator or whatever name you prefer)- Share with us what is being said about the scope and future of Spirituality in the Entrepreneurial Business world.

Unfortunately these days, the business world is about profit, accumulation of wealth in many instances at the expense of others. Unless this trend changes, we will be all losers in the end.

* * * * * * * *

Dr. Carolle Jean-Murat is a board-certified gynecologist, a medical intuitive, award-winning author, and international speaker. She is the founder and medical director of the Dr. Carolle's Wellness Center for Midlife Women in San Diego, CA, which integrates preventative, holistic, and conventional health care and intuitive counselling for women during peri-menopause and menopause years.

She is the author of Mind, Body, Soul & Money: Putting Your Life in Balance, and the award-winning Menopause Made Easy: How to Make the Right Decisions for the Rest of Your Life.

For more information please visit http://www.drcarolle.com or call 619-583-5061.

Take a look at what Dr. Carolle is doing around the world. Visit http://www.supporthtcf.com

"Everything you need you already have. You are complete right now, you are a whole, total person, not an apprentice person on the way to someplace else." -- Wayne Dyer

---

David Chandler

1) New information reveals that 75%+ of the worlds most successful people are profoundly spiritual in both belief and practice. Describe how your personal and business success has evolved through Spiritual Influences.

I have a confession to make. I know my essence is spirit, yet much of the time I don't feel very spiritual!

But I have glimpses of what I believe is my Higher Self and I know that the more connection I make with my spirit, the more success I enjoy. And the journey is so fascinating!

I grew up in a religious environment but at College I rejected religious orthodoxy. However, I continued to seek for an answer to the mysteries of life. And after quite a search I found meaning in a broader view of spirituality.

At the same time I struggled with the concept of money. Money was always an issue in my family. Whilst we were comfortably middle class, there was an underlying attitude of lack and struggle. And religion's attitude seemed to be that money was evil.

I therefore developed the perception that money was hard to come by and that when you did get some you had to hold onto it with grim determination. I also formed the false belief that people who had money were evil and had only achieved their success by exploiting others.

And so it has taken me a long time to come to the understanding that success and spirituality are compatible.

I now recognize that the Universe does not want anyone to live with lack. And that the best way to express your spirit is through success. Because not only does it free you to be the very best you can become but it also means that you can directly assist the most people and, more importantly, help others achieve their potential.

What I have come to appreciate is that the Universe is boundless. Not only in terms of opportunities for success, but also in spirit and love and joy and all the wondrous things of life.

I once was of the view that I could only ever achieve a certain income and a limited amount of success. Now I realise there are almost no restrictions.

Where I once felt love was eluding me, I now know that there is more love available to me than I can comprehend. Where I thought joy and happiness were restricted I have learnt that there are no limits.

And a key lesson is that life is not meant to be a struggle. Rather it is abundant and full of potential and its offerings are there for our enjoyment and growth. So I mustn't grasp after these gifts but learn to accept them into my life with gratitude.

But, there is a catch to all of this!

Whilst I believe the Universe is limitless, I also realise that we can't have everything. And that often we don't understand what we can and can't have!

Our Higher Self knows what the best step is for us at each part of our journey and always seeks to make this clear. Sometimes, instead of what we think we *want*, we get what we *need.*

And while this can be challenging, even frustrating at times, it is also the great joy of life – to discover your purpose. To be on a journey whose destination you can only ever have small glimpses of.

My greatest success has come when I have glimpsed sight of my journey and have aligned my desires with those of the Universe. And so often when I have desperately wanted something and it doesn't occur, I later look back and realise that it wasn't right for me.

So now I no longer struggle. I have confidence that the Universe will provide and I have an attitude of expectancy. Indeed, it is when I am most relaxed and open to what the Universe has to offer that I have the most success.

I have gratitude for what I have and I expect to receive more. Not in a sense that I demand it or need it. And I don't mean that I don't work towards things that I want to achieve.

I just have a quiet confidence that what I need for my journey will show up. And when it does I gratefully accept it – and give thanks.

2) In what ways do you incorporate your Spiritual Beliefs into day-to-day business interactions?

The main belief that affects my business dealings is that *everyone has infinite value.*

So I have value. Those who I work with have value. Our customers have value.

Everyone I deal with in my business has value.

We are all connected via spirit and we are all involved in some way or another on my journey. So the fundamental question I always ask myself before doing anything in my business is, "will this action be for the betterment of my spirit and for those I come in contact with?"

In this context, the cliché of *good service* is irrelevant. Even, "giving value in order to receive" is beside the point.

It just is what I need to do.

Because these people are kindred spirits that have come into my life for a purpose. And whilst they may not always be the kind of person that I would choose to be with, I believe there is a reason for our meeting. Plus there are always lessons to be learnt.

They are therefore worthy of my respect and care. And they deserve the best that I can give. The best products and the best service. Always.

And I need to be authentic. I need to be true to myself and true to those who enter my life and I need to be all I can be in each of those encounters.

The other aspect to this, is in relation to valuing myself and what I have to offer and also being true to myself and my purpose.

For a long time I did work that I didn't like because I thought that was my only choice. I now know differently and am moving to a position where I do not need to do anything that doesn't support me or cause me to grow.

And part of this is valuing what I have to offer the marketplace. I know that my products are good quality and potentially life changing. I therefore value them and do not undersell them.

The final key belief that affects my business is my trust in the abundance of the Universe.

There is therefore no need to force anything or to panic. [Sometimes easier said than done!] Things will happen in the correct order and at the right time.

I know that those who are meant to enter my life as either colleagues or clients will do so and that business opportunities will arise all the time.

Although I must do the work necessary, it should never be a struggle and I need never be fearful.

I just need to be open to what the Universe wants for me. And then go with the flow!

3) What is the single-most important spiritual practice that promotes peace and prosperity within your own life?

I have tried several different spiritual practices but have not found them to be that effective. I still find it difficult to get out of my head - but am working on it!

For example, I have never been that successful at meditation but I do find that quiet focus gives me clarity and direction. This is also when inner peace comes most completely to me.

I seek connection with my Higher Self through intuition. And my intuition is most powerful when I step out of ego; stop trying and just let go.

I have also learnt to trust my gut reaction as the clearest indication of where my journey is taking me and of who to trust or pay attention to.

When I am on my path I am aware of a quiet yet definite assurance deep within me. It is not something I create artificially. Way beyond positive thinking, it is an affirmation of my spirit.

And the most amazing coincidences [with a capital K] appear before me. The exact person, opportunity or event that I need in my life at that precise moment manifests before me. As if the Universe turned its whole attention on me.

Another aspect of my spiritual practice is to avoid negativity and to seek out positive, life affirming experiences. So I avoid negative influences. I don't read newspapers or watch the news on TV. And I avoid negative people.

Instead I surround myself with books and recordings that promote personal and spiritual growth and with people who have a positive attitude and an entrepreneurial spirit.

This helps keep me on my path, as it is too easy to follow the spectators down the side road and too important to lose my direction.

4) Imagine you are having a conversation with God (or the Universal Creator or whatever name you prefer). Share with us what is being said about the scope and future of Spirituality in the Entrepreneurial Business world.

The Universe has always supported and nurtured the entrepreneurial spirit. And it always will.

Those who seek growth (almost a definition of the term entrepreneur!) will always be supported by the Universe because growth is the fundamental goal of the life force.

And entrepreneurs are the creators, the form givers. They take ideas and energy, the two powerful building blocks of the Universe, and give form to their dreams.

But, this growth must be life affirming. Or else it is a contradiction.

So whilst some may use their power to exploit others, their growth will be limited and their success hollow. On the other hand, those who seek growth both for themselves and for those who they meet, are the ones that will achieve true success in both business and, more importantly, in their life journey.

Indeed, it is by this process, that the Universe achieves *its* purpose.

But the entrepreneurial spirit is not for all. You will always be in the minority - but your influence will be great!

5) What is success?

There are two aspects of success. And both of them are about your journey.

If you are on path – you are successful. In other words, if you understand your life's purpose and are moving towards it, you are a success. And if you don't yet know your purpose, aim for goals that express your core beliefs and you will discover purpose.

The second aspect of success is a state of mind. And whilst you can claim this at any time, ultimate success is *freedom*.

Freedom to do what I want to do. When and where I want to do it. And with whom I choose.

But please don't misunderstand me. I do not mean this in an indulgent way. I mean that you achieve definitive success when you are doing exactly what you should be doing at every moment.

And to achieve that in our society requires financial freedom. But for a long time I thought that was beyond my grasp. It was not until I met my first success mentor that I thought freedom was possible for me also.

Now I am well on my way to achieving financial freedom but it has taken 5 years of concentrated action.

The interesting thing is that after the first few years of effort, the growth has been exponential. It seems that once you achieve enough momentum on your own the Universe steps in and carries you forward.

But the key to momentum is passion. Find what it is you truly want to do and then just begin it. More importantly, find what it is that you feel you *must* do.

Find your passion and your purpose. Take massive action. You will achieve your dreams.

Enjoy the journey!

* * * * * * * *

David Chandler
http://www.StockMarketGenie.com
Ordinary People Making Extraordinary Profits!

So many of our dreams at first seem impossible,
then they seem improbable, and then, when we summon the will,
they soon become inevitable. - Christopher Reeve

Susie and Otto Collins

Spiritual Evolution and Influences

Today, we are successful relationship coaches, authors and seminar leaders. We've co-authored several books and courses on love and relationships and we've written a marketing book and an audio course for Holistic Health Care and Body, Mind and Spirit business owners. We are also married business partners.

Our personal and business success is totally synchronized and congruent with our personal and spiritual beliefs and practices.

But the truth is that it wasn't always this way.

Many years ago, our spiritual beliefs and practices were something that were completely separate from business—business was business and spiritual practices were for another time and place and other parts of our lives.

Otto sold radio and television advertising for nearly 20 years and Susie was an educator and librarian in a university system for 30 years.

During those years, although Otto wouldn't have said that he was being guided by his spiritual beliefs, he was to a certain extent. He would never sell something to anyone if he didn't believe that it was in their best interests. In fact, he would put what was in his customer's best interests ahead of the sales goals that were set for him.

Although, in a sense, Otto lived his spiritual beliefs, he hadn't yet made the connection that he could be true to his spiritual and personal beliefs and produce win/win business transactions with everyone he came in contact with.

As his spiritual beliefs evolved, his career began to shift and evolve as well. He got to a place where he was no longer willing to spend his time doing work just for money. He wanted to do work that could satisfy his soul, make a bigger difference in the world and at the same time, give him the ability to satisfy his financial wants and needs.

When he became an entrepreneur, starting his own business with Susie, he realized that he could create the life he wanted, that it's an abundant universe and in business relationships, everyone can get their needs met in an abundant way.

For many years, Susie had the belief that she had to act in a certain way at her work and another way in her private life. Although she always tried to act from Christian values and strong family influences of what was "right" and "wrong," her growing sense of spirituality was something that was practiced primarily outside of the workplace.

During the last few years before she left the university system, she began making the shift at work from having the attitude of merely "doing a good job" to living each moment with a sense of purpose that she is here to make a difference in the world. She allowed this sense of purpose to deepen when they started their business together and it continues to expand and grow.

Day-to-Day Spirituality in Business

Today, in our relationship coaching practice and business, everything we do in general must pass the "Is this in alignment with our personal and spiritual purposes and beliefs?" test before we decide to do it. Since this is a business and the intention is to make money doing the work we love, what we do is find the overlap between our life purposes, our joint mission and what our prospective customers and clients need and want.

As a result of living and creating our business in this way, we have a solid but flexible framework to create all of our products and services that we offer to the marketplace.

We are choosing to create our lives in such a way that there is no separation in any part of our lives. We are choosing to live from our spiritual purposes, as we understand them, every moment of every day. This is what we also recommend to others who want the recipe for success in any part of their lives.

What we have discovered is that you can go to the mountains and caves and meditate like a monk for 30 years, but when you come out, you still have to be with people and live in this world. Because of this, we believe that relationship is one of the greatest ways that we grow spiritually, if we are open to the lessons. We are constantly doing what we know about having a great relationship and learning new ways to connect with each other at a deeper level, as well as connecting with our Creator.

We've discovered that, in our relationship, we have a pretty accurate business success barometer. When we are close and connected, our business success reflects it. As crazy as it sounds, when there are problems, challenges or conflict between the two of us, we become disconnected and our sales figures usually fall.

We've learned that if we want to continue being successful in our business, we have to "walk our talk" in every moment of every day.

Another way we incorporate our spiritual beliefs into our day-to-day business interactions is that we teach holistic healthcare and body, mind, spirit business owners how to market themselves and still stay true to their personal and spiritual path. The reason we do this is that so many people have a mistaken belief that you can't be successful while you're "doing God's work." We feel that it's also one of our missions to help dispel that erroneous belief.

Single-Most Important Spiritual Practice

Our single-most important spiritual practice that promotes peace and prosperity within our own lives is our moment-by-moment focus on what we want rather than what we don't want, while living our purposes and mission.

By aligning our thoughts, words and actions with who we really are at our core, while healing old wounds and empowering ourselves to be who we were created to be, we are creating an abundance of love and money and at the same time, helping others to do the same.

A Conversation with our Creator

If we were to have a conversation with God about the scope and future of spirituality in the entrepreneurial business world, it would probably center around the idea that each of us has the power and capacity to be conscious creators of the lives that we want.

We would probably discuss the idea that no matter what has happened up until this moment, by focusing on what we want verses what we don't want, we can align ourselves to having what we really want and what can make a difference in the world.

We think God would share with us how we can use our own gifts, talents and abilities to be beacons of light for others who may need it. We also think that God would tell us that there is no separation from what happens in the entrepreneurial business world and other "worlds."

In this conversation, we also believe that God would tell us that all work is spiritual work and if you are living your purpose, your contribution no matter how big or small, is vitally important to the success, happiness and well-being of the planet.

* * * * * * * *

About Susie and Otto Collins

Susie and Otto Collins are Happily Married Relationship Coaches and Authors, who are committed to helping other people create more conscious, connected, loving relationships of all kinds.

Together, they are the authors of the books, "Should You Stay or Should You Go?","No More Jealousy," the "7 Proven Secrets For Attracting Your Perfect Partner" course and several other books, courses, articles and programs.

To start getting their free Love and Relationship Gold Newsletter send an e- mailto:joinnewsletter@collinspartners.com

Susie and Otto's Relationship and Personal growth web sites include--

http://www.RelationshipGold.com
http://www.collinspartners.com
http://www.StayorGo.com
http://www.RelationshipTrust.com
http://www.NoMoreJealousy.com
http://www.Communication-Magic.com
http://www.PersonalGrowthPlanet.com
http://www.PerfectPartnerNow.com

Otto Collins is the author of the book "How To market and Promote Your Holistic Heath Care or New Age Business Like a Pro" available from http://www.NewAgeMarketingTips.com

"Happiness cannot be traveled to, owned, earned, worn or consumed. Happiness is the spiritual experience of living every minute with love, grace, and gratitude." -- Denis Waitley

---

Jan Eden

1) Describe how your personal and business success has evolved through Spiritual Influences.

I am evolving spiritually through the following practices.

My greatest practice is consciously choosing to succeed instead of living in wishing and hoping. By choosing to succeed, I deliberately create a clear plan of action. One must first know and feel what it is that makes them successful. If you do not have a clear picture in your mind's eye of what you want, you inevitably get what you don't want.

Success is relative.

Once this is realized, financial success is only one piece of the entire success mosaic. Money is pure energy. Like water, it is intended to flow. We dam our own flow with our lack of belief in ourselves. That lack of belief usually comes in the form of self-doubt - doubting that we have the ability to be as prosperous and happy, as we desire.

Being in business is about spiritual growth, making money is the bonus. By knowing my strengths and perceived limitations, I build a plan of action to heal all aspects of myself that do not serve me i.e. fear of loss, fear of not being good enough, not having enough etc. etc. As I spiritually develop from the inside out, I accept that I am already successful. My objective is to sustain this feeling. As I focus on feeling successful, I raise my vibration. As my vibration rises, I then attract what I desire. We inevitably attract what we feel about ourselves.

I sustain this higher vibration daily by taking personal, professional and financial inventory of what is working in my life instead of focusing on what is not working.

As I take inventory, I am immediately consumed by the greatest of all blessings, an intense feeling of gratitude. I am grateful for what is working and what is not working, as I am creating both.

An example of how I incorporate this belief into my day-to-day interactions is as follows:

When I attend any corporate function, before I arrive, I decide what it is I want to experience from the event, i.e. attract quality clients and new friends. At the same time, I decide what I want to give to the room and what I want to leave behind.

What I want to give is to help someone with a genuine referral, contact or business coaching without any conditions. When I offer a referral, I call my referral or contact after I have passed on their name to let them know that a special person will be calling them whom I met at such and such a function. My referrals and contacts know that I do not network; I purposely set out to connect people to people as most people do not have the confidence or knowledge to market themselves.

What I graciously leave behind is an act of kindness. My offering of kindness has no conditions. I learned a long time ago that there is no competition. When you genuinely believe that what you offer to another without conditions is the best, how can you then determine who is better. I choose to give everything away as I have no fear of loss. Fear that someone may steal my idea or take advantage of me in anyway. I invite them to take my suggestions, ideas and successes and use them to better themselves.

I purposely position myself somewhere in the room and remain stationary. Since I have entered the room with intention, I know I will attract what I came to experience. When practicing this spiritual exercise, I have always attracted the most amazing people on the planet. Meeting people for personal or professional reasons should be effortless. Most enter the room only wanting for themselves and forget what it is they can give to the room and what they can leave behind.

After I leave the room, I reflect on who I had the privilege of attracting and feel such gratitude for the experience. I also reflect on what I may have missed or not paid proper attention to.

For example I attended an IT banquet a few years ago and before I entered the room, only knowing a few people, I declared that I would attract the most fun table to sit at. As soon as I crossed the threshold the host of the dinner immediately introduced me to a table of amazing people. We spent the entire evening laughing and having a great time.

When I left the dinner, I sat in my car and remembered the evening giving thanks for the people I had the privilege of meeting. In my reflecting, I remembered a gentleman who introduced the dinner speaker was moving to Calgary from Ottawa. I recalled his introduction to the speaker, it dawned on me that he was just moving with his young family and that he would definitely appreciate meeting new friends.

The next day, I took the liberty of tracking down this gentleman's business number. I called him and left a message that went like this " Hello David, we have not been formally introduced but I had the pleasure of watching you at the IT dinner introduce the Keynote speaker. The reason I am calling is to ask as to whether or not you have been introduced to Calgary hospitality. If not, I would like to invite you to a special luncheon that I am putting on in your favour. I have several exceptional people that I would like to introduce you to who I know will make your transition to the your new home much more hospitable. If you would like to take advantage of this kind offer, please call me at ……."

David called back ten minutes later and said that "no" he had not yet been introduced to Calgary hospitality and would be honoured to come to lunch.

That was almost two years ago and till this day David and I are special acquaintances.

There were 300 hundred people at the dinner. Why would 299 others not see the benefit in treating a total stranger with such grace? I believe they just do not know the value of honouring another on such a spiritual level. "Do unto others as you would have them do unto you." We say the words, but do we live them?

Like all of us, I too am in process to becoming spiritually greater. I feel privileged to be of service to another and that I can support them in some special way. That is who I am.

I attribute this spiritual practice to my professional sustainability. I know no matter what may occur that I will graciously attract even greater business opportunities.

The single-most important spiritual practice that promotes peace and prosperity is" Living in a State of Gratitude".

My conversation with God is asking for guidance to lead by God's example. In my limited understanding I believe God's example is loving without conditions, love thy neighbour as thy self and be love not fear and choose to live in an a constant state of gratitude.

Translating this into a business context would be to give to each client beyond what they have initially paid for or expected to receive.

Love thy neighbour as thyself, which is the golden rule, is demonstrated through respecting and honouring all who cross your path in business and otherwise even if they appear to be your perceived competition.

Living in the energy of love not fear is knowing that fear depletes your spiritual ability to manifest in the moment. Fear is an illusion and the only energy that will overcome fear is loving first yourself. Until you see your own value it is very difficult to see value in another. For some reason our traditional spiritual teachings have not embraced this huge spiritual truth. We must see our value and accept ourselves without judgment and work each day to consciously improve ourselves not remain in mediocrity. Choosing to be mediocre is a choice. Knowing we have a choice why settle for less. As we evolve and know our own value we effortlessly attract to us a reflection of ourselves. If we love ourselves, we attract others, who love themselves, if we feel we are successful we attract others who feel they too are successful.

Our first spiritual goal is to eliminate all illusions of fear and replace them with the truth that we are worthy to experience heaven on earth. Heaven being a place within us that knows who we really are, and why we have chosen to be apart of this earthly experience. We allow our fears to distract us from our true purpose. Our true purpose is to be unconditional love and by vibrating at this highest energy level we become immune to fear. Can you imagine a world, your life without fear? Would that not be heaven?

Many people are beginning to wake up to their own spiritual understanding. There is no right or wrong way in becoming spiritually evolved. All spiritual paths lead to the same destination; God.

My advice to all entrepreneurs and business enthusiasts would be, that in order to sustain success, one must first trust and believe in oneself. If we listen to ourselves like we have never listened before, we will hear or feel a wee voice deep inside guiding us each step of the way. If we will only take the time to listen.

We are not alone on this short earthly journey. All we have to do is call forth what it is we want to experience and instantly we have spiritual assistance. Hence, the cliché "Be careful what you ask for". It is not trusting that what we have called forth will in fact manifest which challenges the outcome. The greatest secret about success is once we realize that every experience regardless of the outcome is a successful one, our lives take on a different momentum and form. There are no mistakes, only experiences. We chose to become conscious of what serves us and what does not serve us.

* * * * * * * *

Jan Eden, President and CEO of CEO In Training Inc. As a business advisor for the past 25 years, Jan coaches executives and business owners "how to" inspire not manage. Jan is a published writer, international speaker, and author. For further information, please visit http://ww.ceointraining.com

Never doubt that a small group of thoughtful citizens can change the world. Indeed, it is the only thing that ever has.
- Margaret Mead

Stephanie Frank

1) New information reveals that 75%+ of the world's most successful people are profoundly spiritual in both belief and practice. Describe how your personal and business success has evolved through Spiritual Influences.

As a young entrepreneur, I tried to push my way to success, regardless of the circumstances, signs or obstacles in my life. As I grew older and wiser, I realized that I was (and always had been) divinely guided to exactly the places in my life that I was supposed to be. Events occurred that while I once saw them as a failure, served to protect me from choosing a path that would be wrong for me. Today, I "tap in" to that spiritual source every to assist with decisions, make intuitive choices and lead a peace-filled life.

2) In what ways do you incorporate your Spiritual Beliefs into day-to-day business interactions?

Every day, I set out to be heart-centered and to look for the greatness in people. I practice grounding and meditation techniques to relieve stress, accomplish tasks and goals, and get through the day as productively as possible.

3) What is the single-most important spiritual practice that promotes peace and prosperity within your own life?

The time I take to rejuvenate is probably the single most important part of my life. I meditate daily, and give myself breaks free from phones, email and work-related items to clear my mind and help my subconscious work on problems that I have given it to solve. You know how people say they "get their best ideas in the shower?" I do things in my life that take my mind off of problem solving mode intentionally to get those great ideas to come to the surface of my conscious mind.

4) Imagine you are having a conversation with God (or the Universal creator or whatever name you prefer)... Share with us what is being said about the scope and future of Spirituality in the Entrepreneurial Business world.

The Universe is ever-present in creating a new paradigm of business practice. It no longer serves us to be in the "climb to the top no matter what" kind of mode that older business has set its foundation upon. Instead, we are learning to let go, to trust, to collaborate in ways that haven't been taught to us in our school system. While many are unable to let go, there are many others who are thriving in this new, collective environment. The shift to work together is strong, and we must put aside personal ego in order to make the most of this new paradigm.

* * * * * * * *

Stephanie Frank, The Accidental Millionaire
http://www.StephanieFrank.com
sfrank@StephanieFrank.com
Helping Entrepreneurs Find Million Dollar Success
Do you have what it takes to bring health, wealth and happiness into your life? Take our short quiz and find out.

"There is a thought in your mind right now. The longer you hold on to it, the more you dwell upon it, the more life you give to that thought. Give it enough life, and it will become real. So make sure the thought is indeed a great one." -- Ralph Marston

---

Carole Friesen

1) New information reveals that 75%+ of the world's most successful people are profoundly spiritual in both belief and practice. Describe how your personal and business success has evolved through Spiritual Influences.

I believe that to be successful in all areas of my life, I must believe in myself. This comes from many years of exploring my inner world to find my true power of my spirit. I believe that the seed of who I am is planted in my womb where my intuition lays waiting for me to trust in its guidance. There is a pilot light or life energy source in all of us just waiting to be fuelled through unrestricted breathing patterns to take us to a higher level of Being. The resistance to taking in life fully comes from past patterning created from the mind to protect our emotional or vulnerable female side. As we let go of the resistance to change and allow the true power of our spirit to shine through our personality or aggressive masculine side, it reflects into our outer world. In other words, to reach our peak potential of our outer world, we must access our core potential of our inner world which influences everything we do.

"To reach way up, you've got to dig deep down!"

2) In what ways do you incorporate your Spiritual Beliefs into day-to-day business interactions?

I work within the context of my boundaries set by my personal Code of Honor. First and foremost, I must stay true to my heart and to speak my truth with compassion. I feel that the more I trust myself, the more I am open to trust others. I am learning that my word is gold and to only make commitments that I intent to keep. I feel that when I am in Integrity with myself this is reflected into my day-to-day business interactions with others.

"My choices create my reality!"

3) What is the single-most important spiritual practice that promotes peace and prosperity within your own life?

The single most important practice that brings me peace and prosperity is connecting with my Inner Child. When I love and encourage her to grow in all areas of her life, this helps her to move through her fears that she has developed over the years. I look to her for guidance and my life directions. In her innocence, I find my passive female strengths and intuition. She is my G.U.R.U. "Gee You Are You". As I breathe life into her inner world it brings me peace which allows me to breathe life into my outer world of prosperity.

"Just look into the eyes of a child and you will find true spirit!"

4) Imagine you are having a conversation with God (or the Universal creator or whatever name you prefer)... Share with us what is being said about the scope and future of Spirituality in the Entrepreneurial Business world.

"My dear child, I have made you in the likeness of your mother "Earth". Dig your roots deep into the core of her energy, which is fire. Through her warmth, beauty and compassion, you will find what your true natural gifts are. The more you open the doors to her mysteries and wonders, the more I can transmit my light into everything you manifest in your point of balance through the Heart of who you are. You are a conduit of my consciousness of Love, stay grounded in this energy and I will come to you, which will reflect the power you have to change the Universe. You have come from Love and you will return to Love, it is how you use this energy in every moment in between that creates your reality."

"The future Entrepreneurs that allow their creativity to flow in harmony with the manifestation for the evolution of mass consciousness to shift to a higher level of being will benefit from the fruits of their labor at all levels."

"As above, so below!"

5) How do you see Spirit?

I see Spirit as the energy life source flowing through the material world. In nature or mineral kingdom, there is limited consciousness manifesting through the ebb and flow that is constantly learning to find balance within its cycles. In the animal kingdom, we see a limited group consciousness of aggressive and passive nature within each species. In the Human Kingdom, we are of individual consciousness that make up the mass consciousness of our World. In this third dimensions of duality, we have a choice to work with the Spirit of Love to evolve it into a higher level of reality in our own lives and as a Whole.

As Human beings, we have a physical container that is the manifestation of our actions and reaction of our mental (flesh) and emotional (fluid) bodies. Through the study of the Body Mind we have a measure of how the Spirit or life source is flowing through each and every one of us.

I do it through studying and teaching Body Mind Analysis, Face Reading and Emotional Anatomy. I study human behavior patterns through body language and profiling personality potential.

***"When you understand yourself to the core,
you can stand under everything you do in Life."***

* * * * * * * *

Carole Maureen Friesen
Master Practitioner of Psychosomatic Therapy & Body Mind Analysis

Core Potentials Training
"The Art & Science of Face Reading" Workshops
403-329-9356
carolef@telusplanet.net
http://www.threeheartscompany.com

"Every memorable act in the history of the world is a triumph of enthusiasm. Nothing great was ever achieved without it because it gives any challenge or any occupation, no matter how frightening or difficult,a new meaning. Without enthusiasm you are doomed to a life of mediocrity but with it you can accomplish miracles." Og Mandino

---

Gary Gradley

The evolution of my personal and business success through spiritual influences.

Over the last 5 years, I have gone from a hyper, self-centered, fear-based, anxiety ridden individual with a 10 year marriage on the brink of separation/divorce to a more relaxed, giving, trust-in-life oriented individual with long period of peace and acceptance with a healed happy marriage.

I am very grateful for this transformation which continues (there is work to be done on ourselves everyday) which is 100% rooted in spiritual influences.

Five years ago, I became a Christian, surrendering my life to Jesus Christ. After searching for peace for a few years, everywhere from NLP to personal development seminars, to new age healing, to traveling to Nepal with advise from monks/lama, the only lasting peace has come through becoming an active Christian. The resentment and fear that I deeply held for over 10 years was literally washed away, through my repentance of past sins and my deep desire for healing and relief from my mental and emotional anguish.

My personal relationship with the Devine, with God and specifically with Jesus Christ was at an all time high. I experienced long periods of peace and intensively beautiful, loving blissful feelings that always brought tears to my eyes, during deep communion through daily morning prayer time.

So the first Spiritual Influence I experienced was deep redemption and divine peace that surpasses all understanding and description.

The second spiritual influence I experienced was forgiveness; forgiveness of others who had deeply wounded and controlled me in the past. I had attempted to forgive in the past, but was only able to do so partially. Now I was able to forgive 100%, a great sadness had been lifted from me. This total forgiveness enabled me to love again, oh what a difference it felt to want to love, versus the emotional pain of withholding my love as I had done for years.

One night, about fours years ago, I had a profound spiritual experience. I clearly heard in my thinking and felt deeply in my emotions consumed by the spirit, a commandment and expectation that I was being called to play an important role in helping thousands of people choose and be love over fear. In my tears of gratitude and bliss, I accepted this assignment and responsibility of pro-actively educating myself and others in this critical transformation from fear to love.

So the third spiritual influence I experienced was love.

Knowing & feeling that I am in God's love and being ever grateful for my healing and transformation, I became eager to help others in their healing. My relationships with others has broadened and deepened. I am driven to help those underprivileged in dire straights, whose future looks hopeless. I sponsor three World Vision children, contribute money to world crisis situations, and regularly give to the homeless and beggars in the city. Even when it is difficult for me, I can't help but give including 10% tithing at my local church.

So the fourth Spiritual influence I experience greatly is Giving.

My healing, which occurred totally through divine intervention, motivates me to pray for other's healing. I have joined our church Healing Prayer Team that prays through intercessory prayers (interceding for others on their behalf) for others in need with physical, health, mental, emotional, financial and spiritual challenges and illness. I experience deep empathy and sympathy for these hundreds of people that we pray for over the years. I feel very grateful that I and my family don't have any of these major challenges, some life threatening.

So the fifth Spiritual Influence that I experience is actively praying for others, and their healing.

I have found "Theophostic Healing" (Healing through God and the Holy Spirit) to be the most effective and complete. Healing through the Holy Spirit uncovers previously unrecognized, hidden root causes and experiences that are the source of many spiritual, emotional, psychological and physical ailments.

Working with a life coach supported by spiritual healing by a therapist/counsellor has enabled me to heal several important areas, including forgiveness of my father (who died four years ago), which had led to an improved relationship with my own eight year old son.

All these positive experiences that have a spiritual influence have enabled me to truly Trust in Life and Trust in God. Knowing that I am called to do God's work and that God is helping me to make a major transition (even though it seems very slow at times). A transition from working for achievement to working to truly make a difference in 1,000 of people's lives each year.

To totally surrender all of our own (ego-based) control to God's will, living in the divine flow of life by "letting go and letting God" is very difficult at first for most people as I also experienced.

In fact over the period of a few months, I was negotiating with God, God kept saying to me "sell your house" (we owned a $650,000 estate home). My continual response was, "I don't want to sell the house" (I really liked our high quality, spacious living environment). God insisted, "Sell the house," I asked "Why?" God's response in essence was, I can't use you when you are tied to this house (It's true, I was run ragged keeping up with the yard maintenance and financial burden of high mortgage payments). My desire to be used for God's purposes was greater than my desire for the house. Choosing to be obedient to God's will, we quickly sold the house for a good price, with a long closing date required to purchase another smaller new home, which God through my clients, provided the $20,000 down payment required.

So the sixth Spiritual Influence that is having a profound and peace generating impact for me is, Totally Trusting in God.

I love my "faith statement" which I developed at a personal development seminar, which I repeat daily: "I am grateful for this my Faith Statement: I believe in God & Jesus, the purest highest energy which is love. I believe in God's divine plan for me. I believe that God loves me, protects me and provides for me unconditionally. I choose Love over fear and judgment which gives me freedom and joy. I trust in God, which gives me Peace, I believe in the power of Prayer and I believe in the bliss of gratitude through the Holy Spirit".

This statement reinforces my belief that I can & do trust in God. In fact, I have started another company named "Divine Interventions" to do God's work through. **This reminds me of the Seventh Spiritual Influence of Gratitude & Acceptance.**

Being grateful for all that we have, because we have so much compared to the majority of the world. Being grateful for blessings and good fortune. Feeling gratitude brings deep feelings of love and bliss and acknowledges God for his support. Gratitude is the first level of accepting life, usually the good things in life. The second level I believe is acceptance of what life brings, acceptance of the "bad things" as well as all the "good things". This leads to the belief in the principle of Perfection. If we can accept all life experiences as perfect, then we would experience no suffering. Psychological and emotional suffering is usually from wanting things to be different than they currently are. When they don't change to what we want, we experience dissatisfaction and suffering.

Choosing to believe in Perfection: if we believe in God, if we believe that God is perfection, if we believe that God's will is always perfection and God's will for us is always perfect, than we can logically believe that everything that happens to us is perfect and it always happens for a reason. (part of God's perfect plan). When we accept every experience as perfect then we will be like the monks, we will be at peace. I am still working on perfecting this the seventh spiritual influence of gratitude, acceptance and perfection.

Spiritual Beliefs In Day-to-Day Business interactions

I seek to connect with clients & prospects in a personal & professional way to open the door to explore their spiritual beliefs. I have joined a Christian Business Networking Referral Club as the Chapter Chairperson, providing me with a Leadership role with other business people of a common spiritual belief. I am in the process of living and perfecting these spiritual influences in my business by walking the talk of "doing the right thing" as the leader of our training and development organization. I believe that my spiritual journey – that is where I need to grow and develop is being a strong, principle and spirituality-based Leader, who walks by the talk of the following Spiritual Truths:

Peace of Mind & Acceptance

I have come a long way in accepting positive business and sales results with gratitude and an even keel attitude, similarly, I have learned to accept missed opportunities and lost sales with an attitude of acceptance, accepting the situation to be part of God's perfect plan.

Forgiveness & Non-judgment

I continue to work on coaching our sales people from a holistic, non-judgmental perspective, recognizing that they, like me, are only human. I have forgiven the non-performers for their low sales results and have not asked them to leave, giving them another year to improve themselves.

Giving

Being a straight commissioned sales professional for the last 15 years, 100% of my income is from the accounts that I have developed and sold training & development services to. As such, I tend to be fairly possessive of these accounts and commissions. One of the greatest stretches for me has been to share some of these accounts and commissions with other Sales Reps in our company. It has been very difficult at times, and resist falling back into my traditional habits. Yet I am committed to continue to create opportunities to share accounts and commissions as I am prompted to do so by the Holy Spirit.

I really need to obey the Holy Spirit's prompting in this regard as money is my "Achilles" heel as I am very attached to money and motivated by financial security. This transition from getting to giving has been the most difficult one for me, and continues to be work in progress.

Trust & Expectation

I am pleased to say that my level of positive expectation for positive outcomes in business and sales has always been very high. When I walk into a first time sales appointment, I intend and expect to create a solid relationship that will result in business very soon.

I trust that whatever the outcome is, that it is the right outcome at the time according to God's plan.

Most Important Spiritual Practise?

- Daily prayer & meditation (Yoga)
- Prayer which involves:

  a) Asking for specific opportunities and outcomes in line with my personal & professional goals & objectives.
  b) Prayers of deep gratitude expressing my heart felt appreciation and gratitude for good things (and a few bad) in my life.
  c) Prayers expressing my Love and my intimate relationship with God & Jesus Christ.
  d) Prayers for the healing of others

The Future of Spirituality and Business?

A conversation with God about the scope and future of Spirituality in the entrepreneurial business world.

- the opportunity for deep meaningful client relationships that are based more on spiritual meaning and connectedness
- the heightened importance of Leadership
- Visionary leader – allowing God to co-create the leader's purpose, passion, vision

- more compassion and love-based behaviour which treats employees with more dignity, respect & opportunity
- less competition and more collaboration within and between companies
- more forgiveness, trust and harmonious relationships
- more profit sharing and sharing of the wealth based on a more giving vs. getting mentality
- less fear-based and more love-based behaviour & leadership

* * * * * * * *

Gary Gradley, Divine Interventions

Gary Gradley, speaks from experience in transforming his life from a constant state of anxiety and fear to living in a state of Trust and Love, turning around a 15-year marriage on the brink of divorce to a loving happy harmonious relationship. Gary has been working successfully with hundreds of corporations and thousands of individuals over the last 15 years throughout Canada, USA, and Australia as one of the founding partners of the Delta Synergy Group, a local training and development firm. Gary has spent the last decade dedicating his life to the personal and professional development of others, enhancing their individual, team and organizational performance.

Gary is also president of Divine Interventions, a spirituality-based organization committed to helping thousands of people rediscover the power of Love and spiritual truth in their lives. Gary communicates with conviction, powerfully revealing truth with the integration of experiential learning to maximize revelation, impact, personal growth and application.

He is working on his latest book and life-changing experiential workshop "Called to Love". http://www.deltasynergy.com

"Great spirits have always encountered violent opposition from mediocre minds." - Albert Einstein

---

Pamela Harper

1) Describe how your personal and business success has evolved through Spiritual Influences:

My business is more successful, and personal life more fulfilling, each day as I turn over the making of miracles to the true source. It is so comforting to know, not only am I not alone but I don't even have to wonder if I will achieve greatness.

I do not have to rely on will or wishes to be rich and famous; it is guaranteed by Divine Law. I express my greatest desires in the Field of All Possibilities and the Universe orchestrates the details. I am so blessed.

2) In what ways do you incorporate your Spiritual Beliefs into day-to-day business interactions:

Once I began trusting in the Source of all Abundance to fulfill my desires, my success proceeded at warp speed. I trust that because I have asked to live in Higher Consciousness every big and small event and fortuitous opportunity that flows gracefully into my grateful path is meant to help me accomplish purpose and prosperity.

3) What is the single-most important spiritual practice that promotes peace and prosperity within your own life?

I practice unconditional love both toward myself and others. My ego is minimized as I celebrate the successes in all of us. I am free of judgment. To remain in the Light I bask in the Energy of Love through daily (sometimes hourly) prayer and guided visualization.

And God said, "Ye that are willing to walk in the Light in pursuit of your life's work, are deemed healthy, wealthy and oh so happy."

The only other question that comes to mind is, "Why is Troy's book so vital?" Answer: Thank you so much Troy for all that you are and this most relevant and significant work of genuine heartfelt genius.

* * * * * * * * *

By Pamela Harper, RN, CCH, CAC
http://ww.pamelaharper.com **949-388-2763**

"Everybody builds a dream in their lifetime. Your either going to build your dream, or somebody else's. So build your own!"-- Christopher LaBrec

---

John Harricharan

1) New information reveals that 75%+ of the world's most successful people are profoundly spiritual in both belief and practice. Describe how your personal and business success has evolved through Spiritual Influences.

First, I believe that we are all spiritual beings playing the game of life. And the game of life has many challenges, but they can be broken down into three main categories: money, health and relationship. Name any problem you have and the chances are it will fit into one of the three categories. With that said, I feel that my business success is intimately tied in with my spiritual growth. Let me explain.

When I am aware of the real "me", and when I work within the great universal laws, I find that my personal life is greatly enhanced and that I am more capable of dealing with everyday problems. It is not that the problems become easier, but I become stronger and wiser and, thus, am more able to see the problems and their solutions with more clarity.

When I forget who I am and get caught up in confusing efforts to try to solve a problem, I find that this very confusion leads to greater frustration and helplessness. As I return to the calm center, which is within us all, the problem starts solving itself with my help. Using less than our full spiritual arsenal to solve problems is like watering our garden and standing on the hose. Solving problems, business or personal, have to do with getting oneself out of the way.

Many years ago, I wrote the following:

"Whenever problems seem to get the best of me, whenever I feel them closing in on me, I go to a quiet place that lies somewhere in my soul. I do not reason, analyze or think. Those will come later. I simply go. From this place of silence, I garner strength and

*inspiration to stand firm in the face of fire, to be calm in the midst of thunder. When I emerge, the world has not changed, but **I have**. And in changing, a whole new world is born."*

I find that is as true today as when I first wrote it or thought it. Success, whichever way we define it, whether by money standards, health or happiness standards, is not a game of chance. It springs from deep within us, from our deepest thoughts and beliefs. It has to do with our fears and hopes and it flows eternally from our spiritual center of gravity.

2) In what ways do you incorporate your Spiritual Beliefs into day-to-day business interactions?

I do not have to try to incorporate my spiritual beliefs into my day-to-day, business transactions. My day-to-day, business transactions are a mirror of my spiritual beliefs. We cannot be other than who we are, so we are deceiving ourselves when we say that we are trying to be more spiritual in our daily business activities.

Actually, there should be no difference between our business ethics and our personal ethics. If there is a difference, then we have created artificial, double standards. Personal life and business life flow from the same core beliefs.

If I look out into the world and see business and personal problems that appear to be of giant proportions, I have to go back into my belief system and examine it to find what is it in me that seem to project these problems. I might find unsavoury things such as greed, anger, hate, guilt, unworthiness and such. Rather than blaming the world, circumstances or others, I try to take responsibility for myself and choose to change my beliefs. When I do so, my exterior world starts changing.

In my belief system, success is not having lots of money and things, lots of fame and power, or lots of anything. It is having the consciousness from which all these things flow. By being aware of who we really are, by examining our beliefs and changing them if necessary, we'll find that a new world opens up to us, a world filled with all good things.

3) What is the single-most important spiritual practice that

promotes peace and prosperity within your own life?

When I was much younger, I thought that education would be the answer to all my problems, so I went about obtaining degrees. I collected a good number of them including a summa cum laude degree in chemistry and mathematics, and an MBA among others. But I found that my education, even though it helped tremendously, did not bring real satisfaction. So I put the certificates and diplomas in the bathroom under glass and wrote, "Break in Case of Emergency."

Then I started working with Fortune 500 companies and became intrigued with those who frequent the boardrooms of power and fame. And though a part of me was fascinated, thrilled and even enjoyed the trappings of power, there was something, which I couldn't put my finger on that was missing. My heart and spirit were crying out for something that I couldn't find in major corporations.

Still searching for the "Holy Grail" I became an entrepreneur and built a very successful, multi-national business with offices in the United States, the Caribbean, Africa, India and the United Kingdom. Life seemed good. I traveled the world, wined and dined with leaders of industry and even leaders of countries. I was treated as a prince, but soon it all felt empty and useless.

Wherever I sought for peace and prosperity and happiness, I'd find prosperity without the peace or I'd discover abundance without the happiness. Finally, one day, as I sat on my wife's deathbed (she was only in her thirties when she died), it became clear to me that my happiness, peace and prosperity were not dependent on anything external, but on that which was within me, that which had always been with me from my very first day on Earth.

So I started to look within me and discovered a wonderland beyond imagination. I realized that the one spiritual practice more important than all the others that could bring me peace, happiness and prosperity was the practice of going into the "silence" deep within me. Some call it meditation or prayer; others refer to it as contemplation or centering oneself. I do not know what it should be called, but I think of it as the "silence".

In the great silence within, I become renewed, refreshed and excited to face the physical world. When I return from my moments of silence or meditation, I feel great waves of joy. I feel peaceful, secure and safe. Perhaps in the depths of my being, there is a place of beautiful silence where I meet my Creator and where I find renewal of body, mind and spirit.

Perhaps true success and peace emanate from this silent sanctuary.

4) Imagine you are having a conversation with God (or the Universal creator or whatever name you prefer)... Share with us what is being said about the scope and future of Spirituality in the Entrepreneurial Business world.

In my award-winning, best selling book, "When You Can Walk on Water, Take the Boat", (download a free, pdf copy from http://www.waterbook.com/) I recount various conversations with God, the First Cause, the Eternal "IS" or whatever you choose to call this Universal Power. I am convinced that we all have such conversations from time to time.

In my "Conversations with God" concerning the future of spirituality and business, it became clear to me that we are not little clods of clay, but brilliant beings of light on a journey from "all that was" into "all that could be." Business is a game we play like so many other games. And the funny thing about these games is that we could not hurt one of our fellow players without hurting ourselves.

When we think we cheat someone in our business or personal dealings, we are only cheating ourselves. The good we do we do for ourselves. The evil that we do is ours alone. By being aware of our universal connections, we can develop enlightened lives and businesses and see a world of prosperity, peace and plenty.

5) What hasn't been asked that should have been addressed or answered?

It was my pleasure spending a bit of time with you. Perhaps we shall meet again, and, if so, my fervent wish is that we would both be the better for it. After all, business does not do business with business, but people do business with people. All of us are shipmates on the common voyage of life and we cannot sink our shipmates without sinking ourselves. We need to keep this in mind in all our business as well as our personal dealings.

* * * * * * * *

John Harricharan is the award-winning author of the bestseller, "When You Can Walk on Water, Take the Boat". Get a free PDF copy and sign up for John's free ezine at http://waterbook.com/ or http://insight2000.com Photos of John and friends at http://insight2000.com/pictures

"By logic and reason we die hourly. By imagination we live." - John Butler Yeats

---

Mike Helm

"BE CAREFUL WHAT YOU WISH FOR"

I was listening to a "power-of-positive-thinking" program like many times before.

However, this time I decided I was going to believe. I thought I was a believer before, but there is a difference between understanding and believing. Understanding came after I had listened to enough CD's and read enough books that I could write my own book. But, *using* the "power-of-positive- thinking" effectively comes from believing.

It is only after that moment, (I guess, like becoming born again), when it finally hit me that I chose to believe that I would be able to accomplish anything I desired.

The ability to make a reality out of one's powerful thinking is not what I wish to share with you as there are many others who are doing a great job sharing this already. I want to talk with you about "being careful what you wish for". How many times have you heard this growing up? This is a saying many of us have heard many times before and for good reason. It works and I am living proof.

I am sure that if you are reading this book then you are well on your way to perfecting the stages to get what you wish for and therefore I am convinced I can guide you to your true wishes. Let me start by clarifying that I have the correct background for this job in counselling. I am only speaking from my experience. When the day came where I was able to start materializing what I wanted, I made the mistake of focusing on the wrong things for my future.

I was driving from Victoria, British Columbia to Calgary, Alberta between computer stores I managed. I was trying to decide my future. I had invented an internet technology that a few people around me seemed to believe was possible and worth following through to completion. I was told however, that the chances of success on such a venture were slim to none.

Driving in my car listening to a "power-of-positive-thinking" CD (like many times before), that after two or three hours of listening, I decided to start believing, instead of just listening this time. The man on the CD asked if I was driving, to pull the car over to the side of the road.

In the past, I would have just kept driving.

However, since I had decided to believe at this time...I pulled over. What happened next was so powerful it set everything else in motion. The CD had me crying in my car alone on the side of the freeway. And then, within minutes, had me yelling out loud with a powerful joy and with a power I had never felt before. I decided on the spot I was going to go against all odds and create the company I was contemplating.

I turned the car and drove the 18 hour drive to the heart of the Silicon Valley knowing I did not have enough money to get a hotel or gas to return until 10 days later when my wife would receive her next pay check.

On the drive down, I never stopped imagining the company I wanted. I focused on visualizing what the office would look like. I pictured in my mind the programmers I would need. I pictured the meetings that would be held and signing contracts with the businesses that would want my company's services. I imagined the importance of good lawyers and the complexities of the patents. I dreamt about the long talks with qualified staff sharing their opinions on the project. I reached back into my bank of memories for movies I remembered where things like this happened in order to begin imagining all this into reality.

Arriving in California, I headed to the only place I could think of staying. I met a programmer I had chatted with on the internet. There I was at his door. He opened his door to a completely unannounced guest from Canada - me. When I was done describing my dream, I explained the need for a couch to sleep on. The next day this programmer (now also feeling the effects of my dream), called his programmer buddies and within days I had hired a team of six very qualified expensive coders to start on a project which had no funding. I decided that now I needed the legal paper work to start raising money. So, I called my lawyer in Canada. He informed me that he could not help. But, that he had gone to school with a lawyer that worked with the largest law firm in the world.

When I called the firm the secretary informed me that it would be a couple of weeks before I could schedule an appointment, I could not wait that long. So, I left the security of the couch the programmer had loaned me to sleep on, and drove three hours to San Francisco to visit a lawyer who I had never met or even emailed. Two days later I had convinced a partner in the firm to take me on.

Even though, I had not received funding yet. Something I now understand was against all their rules and that had never done before. Within the next few months I had raised 2.5 million dollars and had the exact company I pictured on my long drive down to California. It was just a matter of believing it all like a child believes in Santa Claus. Oh ya, my wife never had to send money.

So far so good!

A couple years later I walked away from the business. I was making $15,000 per month and worth millions on paper. My face appeared on magazines. I was voted one of the top 40 people in the Silicon Valley to watch. Yet, I was more depressed than I had ever been. My wife and I had separated. I was just going through the motions of being successful but not taking the time to experience it. When I realized that this was not making me happy, I sunk into deeper depression.

When I say I walked away I mean I literally walked away. I left the technology to the investors and did not put up a fight to control any of the projects. I simply decided that I needed to be happy and this business was not the way to my happiness.

I travelled the world perhaps looking for a solution, but, not consciously knowing it. I was so wrapped up in the mess I had created that I forgot the "power" of the principle that got me there - *believing in what I wished for*. It was not till much later that I realized that I could create my happiness the same way I created the business.

Simply by just believing it into reality.

Love, happiness, feeling content, and many more feelings are just a decision and so easy to have if you will just allow yourself.

Here is an extreme example and I am only using this to show the "power" without condoning the example. Imagine two neighbours both named Anne. Both live in identical houses. Both go to the same gym to workout and talk. Anne 1 was always telling Anne 2 how she should leave her husband since he was a waste of space while being unemployed and one who drank to much. Although, Anne 2 knows Anne 1 has a rich husband and a beautiful life, Anne 2 for some reason does not believe Anne 1's advice is valid. Anne 2 notices that even though her life is filled with turmoil she still walks around with a smile every day. Anne 2 never tells Anne 1 that her husband beats her on a regular basis. But, Anne 2 is still able to live with a huge smile everyday. A couple months later Anne 1 who is living her perfect life, cleaning her perfect home, decides to end her life in her perfectly clean bathtub. Why Anne 1? Why not Anne 2? Well, Anne 1 pictured her perfect life everyday. She grew up with her perfect husband and her perfect home in her mind and got it. She was then left with a feeling of what next as happiness did not come with the package? Meanwhile, Anne 2 pictured, focused, wished, and dreamt about being happy with whatever came her way. Anne 1 received everything she wished for and only found emptiness. While Anne 2 just wanted to be happy and cherished everything that made her smile every day. Its apparent Anne 2 should leave her husband and share that happiness with someone more deserving but the point is to: ***"Be careful what you wish for."***

I traveled to Thailand. Once there, I found myself comparing extreme lifestyle differences between myself and people I met there. I was doing everything I imagined and was not happy.

Here was a man that made less that $30 per month happier than I thought I could ever be. I wanted what he had.

I figured it out and it was so simple. *It is the comparison of what expectation we have for our life with what we have at this moment that makes us feel successful or not. It is the comparing we do from our dreams and goals to our realities that may give us our self worth.*

First I thought this meant that our goals should be insignificant so we are always impressed with our outcome. But, that would be a worse fate. It is the believing in our goals and having dreams that make life worth living. So what did the man have that I did not? Different dreams. His goals were to enjoy life, to love, and to be loved by his family. His job was just something to keep him where he wanted to be. If he needed a different job to keep him on track with his dream, the new job would definitely manifest. Yet, at the time he was very much on track.

The problem was not that I had got everything that I had wished for. The problem was that I did not wish for the right things. I pictured myself in long meetings talking about the project because that is what I thought was needed. I imagined the office, the lawyers, and the programmers and received all of it. Meeting after meeting and working long hours. It was everything I pictured so vividly only two years ago.

My goals were focused on the outcome of the company I was to establish and manage instead of the feelings I wanted while doing it all. At the time, I had a business so large I could not walk away. I became a slave to the monster I created. I found myself worth more money than I ever dreamed. I had the vacations, the house, and the cars that came with the lifestyle I created but no time to enjoy them.

Don't get me wrong. There are many people very happy living an almost identical lifestyle as the one I created for myself. My point is not that you shouldn't wish for this type of success. My point is that you should be taking your time designing your future to include the love for the future of your success. Dream of how you will feel sitting at your big desk. Concentrate on your goals by focusing on doing what you love to do, not what you think you need to do.

Your big picture should not just be focused on something of circumstance that came along. Rather look for something new that fits the future you want and that wants you.

It boils down to this...

When you decide to believe and I mean *really believe* that anything is possible then anything is possible. So, if this is true, then why waste the opportunity to randomly create your future around "something" happening in your life coincidently right now? Instead, picture the life you want, focused on the feelings you want.

Try focusing on the love you want to feel.
Picture the pride you will feel everyday.
Dream about the comfort you feel with your loved ones and the love you want to receive back from them.

If there is a business idea you want to focus on, great! But, try dreaming about the enjoyment you will receive and the happiness you will derive from the work, instead of just picturing the work itself.

I know all your wishes and dreams will come true so wish the right stuff into your reality, I sincerely hope I have helped you in some small way with your future.

Ps. I decided to focus on *being* happy instead of focusing on "how" to be happy. It works! I am happily married and on Dec 16th we were blessed by little Michael Tavin Helm Jr. Now my businesses are taking off and our future looks so bright. Find something you love to do and do it. Prosperity will automatically follow if you want it bad enough.

I am hoping to release my book soon. If you wish to be informed of its release please visit our site and send us an email.

Sincerely,
Mike Helm

* * * * * * * *

Mike Helm
http://www.mikehelm.com

"It is neither good not bad, but thinking makes it so."
- William Shakespeare

Les Hewitt

1) New information reveals that 75%+ of the world's most successful people are profoundly spiritual in both belief and practice. Describe how your personal and business success has evolved through Spiritual Influences.

My spiritual involvement began with being brought up in a Christian family in Ireland (at the church of Ireland). As a kid, I went to church regularly and sang in the choir. But I was not a converted born-again Christian.

As I went into the work force – the values that my parents had established and observed over the years have definitely contributed to my own well-being. But I did not have any big lightening bolt moment or anything like that, as some have had. I would say in the last 10-12 years I have come to terms with the concept that there must be a God that developed this entire world.

With all the beauty, abundance and complexity out there! It is absolutely incredible, and definitely did not happen all by itself.

Unknown to me, Charlie Tremendous Jones and Tony Compolo are strong Christian guys. I didn't know this when I booked them to speak at some of our events. I learned lots from them, saw their way of life, their integrity – and that truly impressed me.
It seemed that those types of people were being drawn to me... almost magnetically.

Twelve years ago, a pastor came to me wanting to start a church and asked if I wanted to come along. This little community church in North Calgary started. We went along to this church and absolutely loved everything about it. Enjoyed the music, the flavour. Very comfortable.

Now to today, I had never dreamt of doing a book called The Power of Faithful Focus.

I mean if you had asked me that ten years ago I would have laughed.

Then this guy Charlie Self comes to me, who is now my coauthor. A guy with four college degrees, a history buff, been in a ministry for 25 years – and who knows more about spirituality and the bible that I will ever know. He happens to show up in our coaching program in southern California.

I don't thinks that's an accident. I think people show up when the timing is right when you're open, when your being directed into another phase in your life. I believe this is all happening for a reason obviously.

2) In what ways do you incorporate your spiritual beliefs, practices into your day-to-day lifestyle now?

I start my day with Prayer – and ask for guidance - not the exact results as much. Ask for what you want and you will receive the guidance that will take you where you are meant to be.

Spending a good 10 minutes in the morning just thinking through that and trusting in what I receive. That's what faith is all about. You will be guided. You've got to slow yourself down enough to see and hear the guidance and signs you are being given. They can come in various forms so you must pay attention.

Most of us rush into the day. You probably know people like this yourself. They're going like maniacs first thing in the morning. I have a totally opposite approach to that. I get up early. Before I hit the office, it's been 2 ½ hours of working on my physical, mental, nutritional, and spiritual sides. Most are rushing to shave, shower and then run out the door. I take 2 ½ hours to prepare myself.

Then I'm ready for the day. I see too many guys frantic in the morning. I prefer to ease myself into the day. To be mentally and spiritually ready for it.

The other thing is what we teach, this whole thing about what we call the Quantum Results Quadrant. It's the core of our regular coaching program.

The four components are:

1. **Unusual clarity** – knowing what you want and why you want it. Gods guidance will come into this and give you direction.

2. **Successful habits** – again looking at your own behaviour constantly, honing your behaviour so that you get more efficient productivity. Doing things with integrity at a higher level.

3. **Priority focus** – We call it "what are you brilliant at". I think that's a big part of life. It's discovering your inner strengths. What are you truly gifted at. If you believe that God gifts everybody, you've got to figure out what your gift is. Then you have to find an environment, an arena, where you can fully express that talent unrestricted. That's the biggest hurdle that a lot of people get into. First of all, they never find out what their gifts are. Sometimes they get stuck in a job, and life goes on. For me, one of the biggest impacts we have in the coaching we do, is getting people to see what their gift is. Its life changing for them. It energizes them, it gives them confidence and of course they get better results. Then we teach them how to set up boundaries where they protect that talent. So most of the time should be on the talent.

Currently I have three things that I need to focus more on any other things that I do. It is coaching and speaking and creating products. Like Faithful Focus and the whole series that we're doing. If I spend 90% of my time doing those things then I know I'm maximizing what my greatest gifts are. If I'm stuck behind my desk doing paperwork every day of the week – I'm way off track. And that's what we teach our coaching students... how to change that. Most of them don't know.

4. **Relationships** – picking the types of people you want to spend your time with. Or have a strategic alliance with. What is the calibre of people you want to work with? Remember, you draw to yourself the types of people which you think about.

3) Is there any advise you'd like to leave?

When I was a kid, I found writing was a natural thing for me. I thought writing was dead easy. I enjoy sports a lot. My first incline was to be a sports journalist. I probably would have done really well at that. But nobody took me aside and said well lets take a look at this and lets go meet a couple of successful sports journalists, figure out what they do and ask them questions. If somebody had a done that, I would have shifted careers.

Again, I think it goes back to your parents or somebody in the work place. I think parents have a great responsibility at figuring out what their kid's gifts are, supporting and guiding them. Not getting trapped in the typical school environment.

Figure out what you love. Do what you love. Then develop a purpose for your life based on what those talents are. Look for an environment that can give you the greatest leverage for that.

In the Faithful Focus book – we have something called the faithful life quadrant, which is the core of that book, with basically 2 stages to it. From a spirituality point of view its first part is to know God and then to know yourself. And know your true purpose in life.

That's the first stage. The second stage is: love God - love yourself - love others - love your purpose. It takes it to a whole different level. So that's the core of these books.

* * * * * * * *

Les Hewitt, Best Selling Author – "Power of Focus"
http://www.ThePowerofFocus.ca

Also available... The Power of Focus for Women, The Power of Faithful Focus and soon to be released The Power of Focus For College Students (fall 2005)

"I've found that luck is quite predictable. If you want more luck, take more chances. Be more active. Show up more often."
- Brian Tracy

Jill Hewlett

Spirituality in my personal & professional life:

Spirituality is at the core of everything I do, whether it is personal or professional in nature. What I mean by that is, I live each day with the desire and commitment to discover more of who I am, what I am here for and how I can best offer that to the world. This is an on-going process of internal and external transformation. Each day the perfect people, places and situations "show up" and offer me the opportunity to develop this further.

Regardless of what venue I am in, the task at hand or the person I am with, whether it's in a one-to-one session, speaking to a group or producing or hosting my tv show, my intention is to bring more of myself and what I can offer to the situation. That could be as simple as just listening, being patient, encouraging another along their path, or making an introduction.

The ultimate scope of the universe is beyond my personal comprehension, however, my heart is aware, that there is a vision and purpose inherently and intricately woven into the fabric of life. Therefore staying stubbornly limited to my own personal agenda will prevent me from seeing or grasping the bigger picture and the gifts that go along with it.

As an entrepreneur, it's very important that I remember that life isn't A to Z, it's alphabet soup! When I try to control things, which is virtually impossible to do, I waste a lot of energy and I also lose my ability to be creative! Not functioning from the creative brain, means not being able to access my potential. For my personal & professional life to reflect abundance and joy, I must be operating from that place within myself. Life truly is a mirror.

This doesn't mean that I live without goals and plans, it does mean however that, I am here to play my part fully, in the best way I know how, and the rest is up to a power greater than me. There is a humility and strength in this that blows me away. The best part, it works.

Time and time again, I've found, through the work I do in the field of life improvement and goal achievement, that the same universal principles and laws exist. Regardless of age, background or life path, whether it's a child learning new skills in the classroom or an adult wanting to develop more meaningful relationships or improve his or her professional success, we are all on common ground.

The universe is a co-creative place: when we do too much, we squeeze the life force and magic out of the equation; and when we do too little, life passes us by! Keeping in balance is key, and it's such a learning process! The only way of knowing and appreciating balance is from being out of it! In the process of reacquiring it, we develop strength, tenacity and will power, as well as wisdom, compassion and understanding. It's not so much about where we get to, more so - what we learned along the way! I feel that those are the gems we are really looking for, whether we are conscious of it or not.

The greatest spiritual influence in my life is the inner knowing that life is simple and at the same time, it is a vast, infinite and powerful mystery, to which I am here to play a role and it's a role that only I can play! Regardless of the size, shape or form, each of us is an important and unique link in the wholeness of creation.

I believe that our most fundamental "raison d'etre" is being connected to ourself and from that place, fully expressing our unique talents, gifts, feelings, and insights. Not only do we need to do that for our own personal fulfillment, the world needs that in order to be whole and complete as well.

There is a quote in the bible that refers to our labour as being a gift from God. The gift in this statement can be easily overlooked, unless we understand that living our life's purpose is truly "joy in action". The thing we do when we lose track of time, or would do even if we weren't paid, indicates where our passion and purpose are found.

For many years, I saw business and God as being very separate matters. It wasn't until I realised that doing what we love is where God is expressed through us, was it that I was able to feel good about achieving what may be considered "worldly success" and receiving financial abundance. What I do for a living, is an extension of who I am, it's impossible for me to separate the two. They are one in the same and each shapes the other. That to me is profoundly simple & profoundly spiritual.

The most meaningful way I incorporate spirituality into my business:

There is one simple yet extremely meaningful and effective way that I incorporate spiritual beliefs into my day-to-day business interactions. It is a model that I base all choices, decisions and actions, regardless if they are big or small.

I ask myself, "Will this bring Joy to my Heart?, Peace to my Mind?, and Ultimately bring me Closer to God?" If the answer is yes to all 3, then I move forward enthusiastically! If the answer isn't yes to all 3, then I pause and take a closer look.

Perhaps there is something that needs to change within me, or the situation, in order that it can fit the model. If the change is simple, easy, and FEELS RIGHT, then the adjustment is made. The key however, is not to TRY HARD to make it fit! It just is or isn't. That doesn't make the opportunity or idea wrong, perhaps it's just not the right time or not right for ME.

Speaking of TIME, once I do make a decision or take steps to implement a plan, I also recognise that there is my time and Divine Time. Just like 5 minutes for a child is much different than 5 minutes for an adult. For a child it may feel like FOREVER, if they are waiting to go to play in the park, rather for an adult who is hurrying to finish a project to meet a deadline and only has minutes left before she needs go pick-up the kids, time passes by way too quickly!

Along with God's Time, and God's Speed, there is also God's WILL. I am a person who likes to take charge and feel that I have a fair degree of input and say into matters. However there is a vast difference between my will and God's Will, and we know which one is the ultimate power.

I once heard that G.O.D. stands for Good Orderly Direction. Whenever I look back upon the things or circumstances that I believe didn't go according to "my original plan", I am always amazed that it worked out perfectly the way it needed to. There is a peace in knowing that there is a force out there, which is far wiser than I, and when I allow it fully into my life, wondrous things unfold!

For me, successful business practise is usually more about how I get out of my own way, and let synchronicity and divine intervention play itself out. It's often amazing how great things can happen…in spite of ourselves! My part is to show up, do my best and then let go and let GOD with trust, surrendering to the process. Process is a key word here, as we've all heard "Life is a journey not a destination", and "the journey of a thousand miles, begins with one step". Where ever you are, start NOW, when you look back, you'll realise that you've WON!

Self-care promotes peace & prosperity in my life!

The single most important practise that promotes peace and prosperity within my life is SELF-CARE. I can't give what I don't have. That's the bottom line. When I ensure that my own mental, physical, emotional and spiritual health are taken care of, then whatever relationship or project I'm developing, or endeavour I am pursuing, will have the sufficient materials to work with!

Stress is "being out of balance"; balance starts within. The two absolute fundamental areas that I prioritise in order to keep my life in a healthy state of affairs are, my nutrition and fitness. When we are simply dehydrated, never mind malnourished, our system malfunctions, we go into reptilian brain and survival is the only thing that matters. Surviving life is not the same as thriving in life! I choose to thrive.

As well, our bodies and brains need healthy, stimulating, integrative movement to keep it strong, flexible, energised, grounded and oxygenated! Most people feel and think a lot better after exercising. Movement changes our body chemistry and physiology. We need to honour the temple that our spirit lives in. I prefer exercise that is wholistic in nature, meaning it moves my body in ways that are natural and promote balance, connection and harmony between my head, heart and body.

When I engage in activities like this, my spirit soars! Some of my preferences include, walks in nature, yoga, dance and simple activities taken from an internationally recognised work called Brain Gym®.

My conversation with God and the view of spirituality in the future of Business:

I deeply believe that life is the gift God gives us, successful careers in which we make significant and meaningful contributions to others, the environment and the planet at large, is part of the gift we give back to God in gratitude for being alive!

In other words, *"God's gift to us is time, what we do with it is our gift to God". Jill Hewlett*

Life is a intricate dance between being/doing, giving/receiving, action/nonaction, when we learn to integrate these two opposite forces we move into a place that I call "Dynamic Reception". We need to be in action to get results, and yet, there is a place within that action that is purely receptive in nature. It is magnetic and holds the space to draw to it, that which is needed at the time. From there results and success naturally follow.

The more clearly we know who we are in our "inner world", the more effective we can be in the external world". When make the significant and pivotal shift from viewing life from an e.g.o perspective (energy going outward), to a more conscious and self-aware position. our insatiable need to have and to control turns into a beautiful expression of creativity and balance…ultimately success on many levels. Who wants a full bank account without a happy heart? Who can have a happy heart when their basic survival needs are in question?

A great example of this is with a client of mine who is the founder of a well-established company in the financial planning sector. When he called me, he was at a turning point in his life and career.

His business had been very successful on a worldly scale, however physical symptoms were calling him to address some deeper incongruencies within himself. After a couple of sessions, it was clear that his heart wanted him to deal with some issues and make some significant shifts in his way of life.

Over the course of our time together, he identified places where he was compromising his truth and not clearly living his beliefs. Once he recognised these inconsistencies, he could then choose to become authentic in his words and actions, in ways he hadn't before. He moved from a place of saying the right things to please clients in order to make the sale, to a place of owning his abilities and the services he was offering, which were good and many! No longer did he sell himself short at the expense of trying to control the outcome, and make things look a particular way, or the way he thought others wanted to hear. Instead he began to enter each meeting reciting the phrase silently to himself, "may only the truth be spoken, and may only the truth be heard".

Amazing results were yielded from this shift! Not only did his business grow in unexpected ways on a professional level, for the first time after many years on his career path, he was finding meaning and fulfillment in living his purpose. He now radiates joy and passion for his work, and of course, his physical symptoms are gone!

It is so vital that we honour and respect who we are and the gifts we have. Many people are trapped by a limiting belief system that says, "I'm not enough", or "I could never do that". These are only beliefs, they aren't the truth. How many times does a child fall down, before they learn to walk? Life is a learning process that takes time, courage, risks, the humility to ask for help and the wisdom to know that we are infinitely more than we could ever imagine.

When we not only value our own personal needs, but we also tune into the needs of others, "win-win" is possible. Does it serve us to succeed at the expense of anyone else? Are we better off when someone is left behind? Creating community spirit and being of service in a way that not only actualises and liberates our own talents, but also greatly benefits the world around us is possible and this is where we are headed. Our future depends on it.

As entrepreneurs, we can "live outside of the box", be creative, think laterally and role-model for the world a whole new way of doing business!

I am grateful to be part of such an important planetary mission.

In the Spirit of Life.

* * * * * * * *

Jill Hewlett
•Professional Speaker (Keynotes & Conferences)
•Individual & Group Consultant for Personal Growth & Goal Achievement
•Producer and Host of the 'Body-Mind-Spirit in Motion' TV series
•Fully Licensed Educational Kinesiologist & Brain Gym® Instructor

Talented as a speaker and facilitator, Jill Hewlett effectively draws out the wisdom, creativity and passion in her audiences. Her inspirational, educational and enriching keynotes and programs address how to become more empowered and successful in the boardroom, the classroom and the living room!

Using simple, fun and easy methods, Jill assists others in achieving their optimal learning, living and leadership potential. Whether you are an individual client, corporation, educational institution, or organization, we'd love to hear from you! Results are immediate and lasting.

To sign up for our free monthly update, "Learn, Live, Lead" go to http://www.jillhewlett.com and click on the newsletter link.

Contact info:
http://www.jillhewlett.com
success@jilllhewlett.com
(905) 713-0194

"Success is not the key to happiness. Happiness is the key to success. If you love what you are doing, you will be successful."
Albert Schweitzer

Jafree

1) New information reveals that 75%+ of the world's most successful people are profoundly spiritual in both belief and practice. Describe how your personal and business success has evolved through Spiritual Influences.

The success I experienced is completely from doing introspection, meditation, and learning from great masters who have found their spiritual Source. It just happens, once you realize the eternal being that we all truly are, there was no need to seek anything outside of oneself for answers. Once I felt that desperate search was over, I could really relax inside and come home to myself. Simultaneously, everyone started coming to me to find out how to call off their longing desperate search in life no matter what I was doing.

2) In what ways do you incorporate your Spiritual Beliefs into day-to-day business interactions?

I use my past experiences of Samadhi to help others in their true deconstruction of their beliefs/ego-identity, and this is what I base all of our manifesting sessions upon. The experience of realizing our true infinite nature puts your mind at ease, and this Easiness gets transmitted into my coaching and teaching.

My goal is not to give you a new belief system or structure, but rather to assist you in untangling your true self from the beliefs you already have so you can see the Divine is here now. To find total freedom is to be free from all beliefs. I feel so passionate when I experience someone dropping their belief system. You experience them being completely free, open and tapping into a very expansive state.

3) What is the single-most important spiritual practice that promotes peace and prosperity within your own life?

Raising your consciousness is the foundation of all progress on the inner and outer world. I would have said meditation alone is the best way to increase consciousness many years ago, however I've found that meditation alone is not enough in this day and age.

People need a more effective way to just walk up to their mind and tame it. This is why I've created the eight habits manifesting routine which of course meditation is one of the 8 habits. The ease and speed at which we can remove our inner obstacles is MUCH greater when we apply all the foundational vibration enhancing techniques in these ancient habits. Go to http://www.ManifestingVibration.com to download them.

4) Imagine you are having a conversation with God (or the Universal creator or whatever name you prefer)- Share with us what is being said about the scope and future of Spirituality in the Entrepreneurial Business world.

The Universe is all energy and consciousness in a changing form. There is no real difference between money and spiritual energy. It is all spiritual energy in the mind of God. Something defined as "spiritual" means your mind is creating an opposite illusion of something "unspiritual" or perhaps "business-like" behind it.

The future is the merging of these two worlds, creating total acceptance of spirituality as a everyday part of the business world. In the mind of humankind tomorrow, there will be no separation between you and the Divine. Many blessings to you.

* * * * * * * *

Jafree

Enlightening Conversations that Create Success!
http://www.EnlightenedBeings.com
Transform your Life in 90 Days with The Manifesting Program!
http://www.ManifestingVibration.com
The World's Greatest Cancer Fighting Anti-Aging Juice!!
http://www.GojiHeaven.com

"Enlightenment is stillness of mind." ~*Papaji*

"The creative power within us makes us into the image of that to which we give our attention. We are of thinking substance, too, and thinking substance always takes the form of that which it thinks about. The grateful mind is constantly fixed upon the best. Therefore it tends to become the best. It takes the form or character of the best, and will receive the best."
--Wallace D. Wattles, in The Science of Getting Rich

Julian Kalmar

The Spirit of Craftsmanship in Business

Being in business for myself is not what I ever would have imagined. I didn't grow up in a business-oriented family, or have formal training in business. My early impressions of "business" were of money-grubbing merchants using every technique imaginable to extract money from the unsuspecting. It was a game of the unscrupulous trying to figure out how to take advantage of people.

The result of my naïve impressions was that every business I tried made only a little money and often lost money. I was never dishonest, but I had no idea what business was all about. All I knew is that I had to do something to get people to hand over their money. My later attempts involved using a spreadsheet. I thought that if I figured out all my costs and selling prices, I could figure out how to extract money from others. I still failed. What was I missing?

What I've finally learned is that if you try to get all you can from others, they will respond by trying to get all they can from you. You will find your business dealings very difficult. A change in spirit, however, yields a totally different response from others and it's their response that yields an easier, more successful business life.

Imagine how easy business would be if your clients did whatever they could to help you succeed. That's how easy my business life is today. Everyone I work with is interested in my success. How did I "trick" them into doing this? It's not a trick, but there is a method to it. It has to do with what I think, and how that thinking manifests into words and actions. I must warn you however, that if you use this method, you will only succeed if it is a reflection of your heart's desire.

First, no matter what you do for your clients, you must understand your position. You must remember that you are a guest in their lives. They don't have to invite you back. Your work for them is not a right; it's a privilege. If they invite you back, it's because you are pleasing in their eyes.

So how should you behave as a guest? You must try to inconvenience your host as little as possible. Then, you must do everything in your power to benefit them. If you cannot benefit them, you must not pollute their lives by your visit. In other words, you either improve their lives, or leave their world unchanged.

Second, you must think in the right spirit. It's really simple. In every moment, you must ask yourself two questions:

- What can I do to help?
- How can I make things better?

Third, you must follow through, both in spirit and in practice. It's not enough to have good wishes for your client. You must take your sincere wishes for them and convert them into actions. In a nutshell, you must deliver. If you say you'll do something by a certain time, you must always do so. If you cannot, you must give your client as much warning as possible so they can plan around your late delivery.

Surprising them at the last minute, or simply not showing up as promised leaves a very bad impression. Would you invite a party guest back who promised to bring the main course, and then not only didn't let you know they couldn't do it, but didn't even show up? Of course not. The same is true in business.

Fourth, how you perform your work for your clients is vital. Everything you do must be of the highest quality. You cannot ever be sloppy. Never let anything go that is just okay. Make it right. Again, the party guest who runs out of mayonnaise and substitutes an industrial glue—because it looks the same—will not be invited back. You must always deliver the highest quality. If you cannot, you tell your client honestly. Say something like, "Jim, I'm really sorry, but I'm having trouble finding the proper lumber for next Wednesday's job. I don't want to give you less than the best, how can we work around this?" Never make an unauthorized substitution. It will come back to haunt you.

I realize that what I've said is very practical on one level, but what drives all this is a deep sense of honor. I'm not talking about honor to show other people what a great person you are. Rather, I'm talking about the feeling you get inside. Just consider how you feel when you try to swindle someone versus when you do everything in your power to help them. Always, it's your spirit of helpfulness that makes you feel the best. Doing a good job is more than a way to turn your clients into your friends; it's a way to gain enormous satisfaction from your work. Every minute you spend delivering quality is a minute of gaining a deep sense of satisfaction. Although your client benefits, it's a gift you give yourself. You have tremendous peace of mind.

What I've tried to give you in a small space is the flavor of what I consider most important. The full spirit embodying these thoughts is described in "Happiness: The Highest Gift," an audio course available from: http://www.thehappinessformula.com. In it, you'll find a much more complete description of "The Spirit of Craftsmanship." These are the lessons I learned growing up watching a master craftsman at work. It took me years to recognize that the spirit of craftsmanship I learned, as a boy was exactly the spirit needed for success in life. I wish someone had drawn this one great connection for me.

If there's a way I can help you in life or in business, please let me know. I wish you the best of success.

* * * * * * * *

Julian Kalmar
Marina del Rey, California
http://www.thehappinessformula.com

"How much abundance that already exists in your life do you take for granted? How can we expect more from the Universe when we don't appreciate what we already have? Today, start to make a spiritual inventory of all your blessings. So much good happens to us, but in the rush of daily life we fail even to notice or acknowledge it." --Sarah Ban Breathnach

---

Mike Lamb

1) New information reveals that 75%+ of the world's most successful people are profoundly spiritual in both belief and practice. Describe how your personal and business success has evolved through Spiritual Influences.

I believe we are all connected. You never know who somebody knows, when they will meet someone that you know in the future, or when they will learn about you from someone you don't know. I believe in the universal Law of Karma where if you wrong someone it will come back ten-fold or more in negativity.

If you do something good, the same thing happens but with positive results.

There's the golden rule then there's knowing the power of the golden rule. We're all spiritual beings and we should treat each other as such.

The evolution of my business success is purely based on the relationships that I build with my guests, customers, advocates and friends. Someone doesn't have to be a believer in spiritual goodness for me to treat them that way. Bringing information, facilitating other relationships, assisting whenever possible is what I do to build my business. With every act I don't think about how this is going to play on the universal stage, nor do I do it because I know there is a profit in it. I do these things because I know it's what I'm supposed to do. My reward is the reaction and the performance of others from my deeds.

2) In what ways do you incorporate your Spiritual Beliefs into day-to-day business interactions?

I treat people the way I think they want to be treated. I do things to make people feel good about what they're doing, about what they're thinking about themselves. I try to encourage and promote to people the idea that little things can empower them to do greater things. Not always or with everyone, but I usually try to suggest or impress upon someone that doing more for someone is always a good thing.

To master the process of empowering people, however, you have to recognize their level of spiritual maturity. By that I mean they have to be open to your suggestions both on a conscious and sub conscious level.

It was recently pointed out to me that my energy, excitement and enthusiasm about what I do also plays a role in my spiritual foundation.

3) What is the single-most important spiritual practice that promotes peace and prosperity within your own life?

Essentially, it's my belief that I can do anything. We all have free will. I have no limitations. Of course, I do. We all do. We each have a beginning and an end.

Our end is a part of our life, but until that day comes, I truly believe that I can accomplish anything.

I believe all I have to do is decide what I want to do, figure out the resources and the people involved, develop a plan, create a proposal, make a presentation and examine and tweak the results. While doing all of this I imagine, I meditate, I pray, I try to connect my higher self, connect with God and access things on a cosmic plane that I can use in the creation of my plan.

In other words, I talk to God in the way I expect God wants to be talked with. I thank him every day for the gift of my life and the lives of my friends and family, my business associates. I say thanks for my imagination, my passion, my ability to relate to people, to build relationships, my desire and ability to help people, my desire to do more than most people, my desire to not be negative and my hope.

4) Imagine you are having a conversation with God (or the Universal creator or whatever name you prefer)... Share with us what is being said about the scope and future of Spirituality in the Entrepreneurial Business world.

As I just shared I do talk to God on a religious level, but also I speak to him on a social level and different spiritual levels. I ask for assistance for the things that I'm doing, the things that other people are doing and want to do, and I ask for strength and guidance so the information that I impart to someone makes a difference.

As I imagine what is possible in my life and in those that I work with, coach and make offerings, I know somebody is listening. Too many things happen for me not to believe them. Like many entrepreneurs I see a great future for business in general, but especially the micro-business people that have so many opportunities if they would just set aside their fears, anxieties and frustrations long enough to tap into their own ideas and imagination which we all share as part of the cosmic consciousness. I feel very bullish about doing spiritual business.

5) What hasn't been asked that should have been addressed or answered?

I think each of us has a responsibility to bring our spiritual life into our business life. Not to preach, witness or wear our spirituality on our sleeve, but to be aware of our actions and the outcome of our work. Do unto others, but be keenly aware that we can easily harm someone by some of things we do. Don't just think profit for profit's sake. Make a conscious effort to realize that some things will be good for us and not good for others.

99% of the time it must be a win-win situation for both parties or there will be dissent and sorrow in the relationship. We all make some mistakes along the way, but it's doing those things we know to be wrong at the time we're doing them, the intention of doing wrong things is perhaps the most unspeakable. Our intent to do "good" is the true power and responsibility in any business relationship. Once we learn that we cannot help but become successful.

* * * * * * * * *

Mike Lamb is a writer, author, voice over talent and marketing coach.

He is host of The Moneyroom Show, the original radio show about web marketing. His audio archives are full of interviews with the most successful people doing business on the Internet.

He publishes a weekly newsletter. To sign up or receive a sample, visit Mike's core website, http://www.moneyroom.com/Mike's email is mike7@moneyroom.com and he can be reached by phone at 316-265-0100.

"If a window of opportunity appears, don't pull down the shade."
- Tom Peters

Dr. Bob Levenson

1) New information reveals that 75%+ of the world's most successful people are profoundly spiritual in both belief and practice. Describe how your personal and business success has evolved through Spiritual Influences.

I would have to say the effectiveness of my professional work definitely has increased the more I allow myself to be guided by spirit. I am more appreciative of the gift of helping people to change their lives that I have been given. It seems this acknowledgment and appreciation is increasing my gift.

Often I get inspired during my sessions and this comes out both in my counselling and hypnosis. I believe that spirit is guiding me to deal with those areas I can make the greatest contribution. Two of those areas happen to be in the smoking and losing weight but more and more I seem to be getting into the area of physical healing as well i.e. frozen shoulder.

In my personal life, I find that I am asking spirit for more help and guidance and it seems to be working. I seem to be doing a better job of parenting and being a loving husband. I am also becoming calmer and developing more patience with my family and this is undoubtedly is leading to more harmonious family relationships.

2) In what ways do you incorporate your Spiritual Beliefs into day-to-day business interactions?

I believe that you reap what you sow. I try and give my best to my clients Customer service is becoming more important to me and that is showing up in new ideas I have, to get the best results for my customers. I also believe that we do possess an inner power and wisdom that can help us to achieve our goals and do the best for our clients. I seem to be listening to that inner voice more and more and I can see that it is leading me on the fast track to increased health, wealth and prosperity.

3) What is the single-most important spiritual practice that promotes peace and prosperity within your own life?

I believe the most important spiritual practice I have is taking time out every day to spend time with God. My daily meditation not only fills me with peace but it renews my spirit and provides me a way to express my gratitude for all my blessings.

4) Imagine you are having a conversation with God (or the Universal creator or whatever name you prefer)... Share with us what is being said about the scope and future of Spirituality in the Entrepreneurial Business world.

Dear GOD, How can I "cast more seeds of love for you on the path of seeking souls" and how would you like entrepreneurs to be more spiritual in their approach to business?

Hello my son... I love when you ask me questions...

The business community is beginning to realize that they have a responsibility to the community, not to just line their pockets with money. All people are my children and I would like to see more integrity and service offered to your customers.

My desire is that you do not sell them on whatever you can sell them on in order to make the most money. I would much prefer you truly take their needs into consideration and give them services or product that are in their best interest. I also would like to see business act in a more charitable fashion. I really am very happy about that Greek restaurant in Calgary who feeds the hungry on Thanksgiving. Could you and other businesses not come up with a similar idea?

For example Bob, consider doing a free stop smoking seminar around Christmas time for those homeless souls who go to the Mustard Seed or Salvations Army. They truly cannot afford to pay for your services and helping them to quit will give them more money to spend on the necessities of life i.e. food, shelter etc. This is truly helping your brother and not expecting anything in return. I can assure you the goodwill and reputation you will receive will surely draw many new customers to you and you will be unduly rewarded both in dollars and more importantly "knowing you have done unto others as you would have them do unto you".

* * * * * * * * *

Bob Levinson – http://www.abc-hypnosis.com
403-255-2273 – Unlock the Power of Your Subconscious Mind!

Life is a leap into the unknown. If you want a guarantee, buy a toaster - Bill Harris

---

Michael Losier

Just Allow? But How?

If you've been practicing the Law of Attraction, then you're probably familiar with the expressions, "just Allow" and "it will come." Well, technically, both expressions are true. However, 'Allowing' is not just thinking that you can have your desire, it's also knowing and feeling that it is possible. When we believe we can have our desire, we have no doubt in receiving it. In other words, we 'Allow'. Simply put, 'Allowing' is the 'Absence of Doubt'.

Understanding this concept makes using the Law of Attraction to deliberately attract more of what you want much easier.

The three-step formula for Deliberate Attraction is: (1) Identify Desire, (2) Raise the Vibration (feeling), and (3) Allow it. Many of us are very good at the first two steps, coming up with the desire and getting excited about it, but the third step is harder. In fact, the Allowing step is the one that needs the most attention.

The thing to keep in mind is that your desire can come to you very quickly, providing you have no resistance in receiving it.

So removing or lessening your doubt - a process called 'Allowing' - is key.

For most of us, telling us to "just Allow" does not help. We need tools to assist us. Here is a tool that will help you lessen doubt whenever you feel it, or hear it, in that little internal voice that we all have.

Let's say, for example, that your desire is to attract your ideal client, or your ideal relationship, and you have a feeling of doubt that it is possible for you. Your doubt or resistance is what is stopping you from 'Allowing' your ideal desire.

To lessen that resistance, ask yourself this question: "Is there anyone on the planet that is doing or having what I desire?" If so, then you now know it is possible. Continue building statements in your mind or on paper that tell you that your desire is possible. Here is an example of an 'Allowing' statement made by a practitioner wanting to attract his or her ideal client:

"Thousands of practitioners have a full thriving practice."

"Hundreds of thousands of dollars were paid to practitioners today, yesterday and will be paid again tomorrow."

"Millions and millions of dollars will be earned by practitioners."

When using the formula for Deliberate Attraction, spend most of you time Allowing, as it determines how quickly, if at all, your desires will come to you.

Use the Law of Attraction to Build Your Business!

Have you ever had something you wanted just fall into place; come to you through an out-of-the-blue phone call or by coincidentally meeting someone on the street? Have you ever met the perfect client or life partner--just by being at the right place at the right time?

Many of us have various ways to describe this phenomenon; serendipity, coincidence, fate, karma, luck, it was meant to be, self-fulfilling prophecy, what comes around goes around, and success breeds success. All of these expressions describe what is known as the Law of Attraction.

Law of Attraction can be defined as: You attract to your life whatever you give your attention, focus and energy to, whether wanted or unwanted.

If you wish to attract more money, referrals, clients, contracts, business partners, or anything else your heart desires, it is essential to understand the workings of the Law of Attraction.

The first step is to know more about our use of Declarative

Statements and how they contribute to Law of Attraction. A Declarative Statement is a positive statement of what we want to attract, which elevates our mood or feeling. Examples include: "I love the way money comes to me effortlessly in expected and unexpected ways." "It feels so good knowing that business comes to me in all seasons." and "I love the way my reputation attracts clients to me."

When people fail, it's often because they have unconsciously made Declarative Statements to themselves that are negative, such as: "Money comes in one hand and out the other." "I take one step forward and two steps back." or "My business slows down during the summer months." These statements have negative feelings and moods attached to them.

Re-read the definition of Law of Attraction: We attract into our lives whatever we give our attention to, whether wanted or unwanted. Law of Attraction responds to these negative feelings and gives us more of them. Law of Attraction does not know whether it is something you want or not; it simply responds to your mood or feeling and gives you more of it.

Each time you hear yourself make a Declarative Statement that does not serve you, simply restate it and offer a better mood or feeling. Here is a quick way to turn a negative statement into a positive Declarative Statement.

Simply ask yourself: "So, what do I want?"

The moment you define what you do want, you start to experience a new mood or feeling, and Law of Attraction will respond to this better mood or feeling.

Over the next few days, start to notice what is appearing in your life, that is, what you are attracting. Then think back to what mood or feeling you may have offered that could have attracted what appeared. You'll soon find yourself manifesting more and more of what you do want, and less of what you don't want, by deliberately putting the Law of Attraction to work for you.

How Can I Tell What Vibes I'm Sending Out?

The Law of Attraction exists in your life right now; whether you understand it or not, whether you know it or not, and whether you like it or not.

Until you learn to use the Law of Attraction in a deliberate way, most of the time you are not aware that you are attracting into your life more of whatever you are giving your focus, attention, and energy to. This is referred to as *non-deliberate attraction*. It can be described in a 4-step cycle:

Step 1: I observe what I'm attracting in any area of my life.

Step 2: While observing what I'm attracting, I'm offering a corresponding vibration, whether negative or positive.

Step 3: The Law of Attraction is always checking in to see what my vibration is and matches it obediently, whether wanted or unwanted.

Step 4: As the Law of Attraction responds to my vibration, I receive or manifest into my life, more of what I was observing in the first place.

Then, the cycle begins at Step 1 and repeats itself over and over again. Here's how the cycle may be working in your life right now.

You may notice that you keep attracting negative people and events into your life. As you notice or observe this, you are emitting or offering a corresponding vibration. The Law of Attraction responds to your vibration by matching it and giving you more of the same. In this example, *more of the same* means that you experience more negative people and events in your life.

Keep in mind; the Law of Attraction is a powerful and obedient universal law. It doesn't know whether you want more of something or not; whether it is good for you or not or whether it is wanted by you or not-it simply gives you more of the same.

If you are curious about what it is you are offering vibrationally in any area of your life, you need only look at the results you are getting in that area, it is always a perfect match. When you observe what you are attracting and you like it, celebrate-and in your celebration, you'll attract more of the same.

When you observe you are attracting something that you don't like, you can use the Law of Attraction deliberately to put a stop to it and change it into something that you DO want. The easiest way to do this is to ask yourself, "So, what DO I want?" and then keep your mind focused on this new clarity of desire. Now you are becoming a deliberate "*offerer*" about what you do want and the Law of Attraction will respond accordingly.

As you continue to practice this, you'll soon be able to check into this area of your life and see the NEW results you are getting.

* * * * * * * *

Michael Losier, a Law of Attraction Trainer and author, supports people in understanding and practicing the Art of Deliberate Attraction; so they can have more of what they want and less of what they don't.

Michael has been applying the principles of Law of Attraction for many years and enjoys a wonderful and rewarding life in the city of Victoria, BC, Canada. He facilitates a number of in-person Law of Attraction seminars as well as Teleseminars to a worldwide audience.

For more articles by Michael Losier, Teleclass information or to purchase the book, Law of Attraction, The Science of Attracting More of What You Want and Less of What You Don't, visit http://www.LawOfAttractionBook.com

"The secret of success is to go from failure to failure without any loss of enthusiasm."
--Winston Churchill

Kathleen Mailer

1) New information reveals that 75%+ of the world's most successful people are profoundly spiritual in both belief and practice. Describe how your personal and business success has evolved through Spiritual Influences.

This has been the most exciting and incredible journey. In the past I would create huge success then something would happen and I would loose all of my effort, my spirit, my energy, everything. I was so unbalanced. Then when I REALLY GOT it, I found some amazing techniques that work with spirit. My business grew beyond my wildest dreams. This spilled over in my personal life. I enjoy a very well rounded and balanced life now. I LOVE my life. This component is definitely "KEY".

2) In what ways do you incorporate your Spiritual Beliefs into day-to-day business interactions?

I incorporate mediation and prayer for my clients/colleagues. I bless them. I ask for guidance to help me be able to help them. I am a very creative person, thanks to my Spiritual Beliefs. I am an author, so of course, my best writing comes from God (my Spiritual belief). I ask for incredible miracles and I receive them. Interesting how simple this is. Another important thing I do is ask God first thing in the morning to send me someone who needs my help. Everyday, I have new contacts or renewed contacts phone, email, fax or just show up! I have never really needed to officially advertise in the past.

3) What is the single-most important spiritual practice that promotes peace and prosperity within your own life?

Prayer. That time to create, breathe and rejuvenate. For me, Jesus is like my best friend. I tell him everything and ask for help in everything I do. For me, there is nothing like this time alone. I get the 'inside story' so that I can best be prepared to help someone out.

4) Imagine you are having a conversation with God (or the Universal creator or whatever name you prefer)... Share with us what is being said about the scope and future of Spirituality in the Entrepreneurial Business world.

Jesus says, "I will build my church"... to me that means he will do it with or without our help. I think spirituality in the business world is excitingly increasing. We are a much more rounded people than we often get credit for. The old ways of business just are not working because we are limiting our success.

In my imagined conversation, I can hear that we are more than limiting ourselves if we miss the spiritual aspect. How? Stress factors? No time to rejuvenate. Customer Service? Not connecting to what your client truly needs and wants...less repeat business. Sales? Not 'seeing' the opportunity when it arrives in front of you. This could be a networking possibility. This could be a new client in the grocery line up. This could even be someone you may be considering 'competition'. You may just find out - if both are willing- the incredible explosion of income, help, and joy that can come from this spiritual aspect. Spirituality IS the backbone, not the component of a good life. When we realize this, the entrepreneurial realm will be dropped on it's ear and intently listening.

* * * * * * * *

Kathleen D. Mailer - The Coaches Coach, Author, Entrepreneur and the Dean/Founder of The Opulence Academy- "Helping Coaches, Trainers, Leaders build their business with MAXIMUM IMPACT!"

Author of Breaking Through Your Business Barriers!, Leadership Wisdom From the Rock: Transform Your Thoughts, Manifest Your Dreams. Creator of: How to Write & Publish Your Own Book: From Conception to Bookstore in 90 Days!
PH: 1-877-751-8037 ext 3 Local Calgary: 403-230-5946 ext 3
E-Mail: opulence-academy@shaw.ca
http://www.kathleenmailer.com

"Money is the most important thing in the world. It represents health, strength, honor, generosity, and beauty as conspicuously as the want of it represents illness, weakness, disgrace, meanness, and ugliness." -- George Bernard Shaw

---

Jason Mangrum

1) New information reveals that 75%+ of the world's most successful people are profoundly spiritual in both belief and practice. Describe how your personal and business success has evolved through Spiritual Influences.

My personal and business success would not have been made possible if it were not for active spirituality in my everyday life and business. Regardless of your belief, spiritual background or religion, you must know and understand that your outer surroundings and circumstances *mirror* your thoughts, feelings and emotions from within.

You can emulate the richest and most powerful people in the world, to a "T." You can copy each and every step another created and applied to make them successful. You can do all these things, and *never* reach the level of success they achieved. Why is this?

It's because your inner-thoughts, beliefs and "mental frequency" is still set to that of the unsuccessful, the poverty-stricken, or the undeserving.

From the very moment I realized this and began to make a conscious effort to affect change from *within*, my entire life took a 180 degree turn. As I changed from within, my outer circumstances changed accordingly.

I began to make better decisions. Better and wiser choices. Why? Because I had trained my mind to eliminate thoughts of fear, rejection, envy, greed and limitation.

***"You are only limited to what you limit yourself."* –Jason Mangrum**

I stopped worrying about HOW I would achieve my goals. Instead, I began to clearly focus ON my goals and intentions – practically anything and everything I wanted to accomplish for that day, that year, that month, etc… You see, when you gain a ***clear*** focus of where you want to be or what you want to accomplish, you immediately begin to direct that energy into manifestation. As soon as you begin trying to consciously control it (i.e. by thinking "how?") your conscious mind or "ego" interrupts this flow of energy, and causes your manifestation to slow down, or deter from its original target completely.

As you are now beginning to realize – *even as you're reading these words* – your "inner reality" controls your "outer reality" 100% of the time. Every event. Every circumstance. YOU control every instance of every moment of your life, from within. It only makes sense to realize and learn to understand this principle of your life. When you realize this knowledge, you'll instantly understand the prime teaching of just about every book, manual or document ever written on personal development, personal achievement and spirituality.

It's that powerful.

2) In what ways do you incorporate your Spiritual Beliefs into day-to-day business interactions?

I practice what is called "active meditation" in my everyday life. From the moment I wake up, until I go to sleep, I am meditating. No, I'm not sitting over in the corner with my eyes closed and legs crossed in the lotus position.

Meditation is focus. The Christian Bible calls it "prayer." It is a clear focus of the divine connection within you.

The Tibetans *live* by this meditation. In both their greeting and passing, they mention it. They call it "Namaste", which roughly translates "In Peace and Love, I Bow to the Divine Within You."

We are all connected to this Divine Source. I won't get too metaphysical right now, but regardless of your belief system or religion – all have one similar connection: To be re-integrated (or rejoined) with the Divine.

Where does all this fit in business, you ask?

Understand this. When you realize this Divine connection, you realize the true meaning of the "golden commandment" taught in every major religion: "Love your neighbour as yourself." For when you truly love your "neighbour" as yourself – and apply this to your business practices – your income will skyrocket.

Why? Because you will begin to always treat others as you wish to be treated. You will go out of your way to satisfy your every customer. Your Joint Venture partners will fall in love with you. Everyone will want to do business with you. You will put your customers' needs and wants far above your own. And this in turn, will open the floodgates for you to receive exactly what you will THEN feel you truly deserve – prosperity.

One of the greatest quotes in our history was "*Know thyself.*"

The hidden meaning of this statement is to make an effort to understand your own human nature, in order to realize the very real connection with ALL of human nature. And one, who understands all of human nature, knows exactly what motivates the mind what inspires the soul and what makes people WANT.

Are you beginning to see the power of this philosophy when applied to business?

It is indeed powerful. More powerful than any marketing "tip, trick or technique" you'll ever learn. I guarantee it.

3) What is the single-most important spiritual practice that promotes peace and prosperity within your own life?

To realize that all rivers run into the same ocean, and all oceans are connected. It doesn't matter what you believe, or what you perceive to be truth. Perception is another aspect of our free will. Manifestation occurs through BELIEF.

The action or application of belief is called FAITH.

When you operate according to a belief, you are operating with faith. Belief is your vehicle of manifestation. Faith is the fuel.

It doesn't matter what your belief is (as long as it doesn't limit you in any way) – what matters is that you apply faith to your belief, with a clear focus of your intended goal. This applies to ALL beliefs, regardless of spiritual practice.

Operate under this, and what I've said elsewhere in this contribution – and you will live in peace and prosperity.

4) Imagine you are having a conversation with God (or the Universal creator or whatever name you prefer)... Share with us what is being said about the scope and future of Spirituality in the Entrepreneurial Business world.

Business practices without any form of spirituality will not prosper.

There can be a time of prosperity, (because there is faith and belief that it will work), but it will surely be short-lived.

This is due to Newton's 3rd Law, which clearly states "For every action, there is an equal, and opposite reaction."

The Eastern cultures often refer to this as "Karma."

There is no good, and there is no evil. There is only existence, and how one perceives what is "good" and "evil."

For instance, you perceive the September 11, 2001 attack as "evil." However, those in the Middle East truly believe that WE are evil, and they are therefore performing an act of "good" to be rewarded by God.

Karma does not see good or evil. Karma simply creates polarity between positive and negative energies, as you perceive them.

If you do something that you perceive (from your belief structure) to be "bad", you will be operating from that energetic frequency. More of the same will follow. Likewise with what you perceive to be "good."

This occurs in the very manifestation of thought itself.

This is why Spirituality and Self-Love is absolutely ***essential*** for lasting business growth and expansion to occur.

You will be seeing evidence of this more and more in the ***very*** near future. Mark my words.

Businesses based on Spiritual practices will flourish. Those that are not, will not. This is Universal Law.

As we begin to enter into a new era of consciousness (foretold in most spiritual texts), this will become much more apparent in every day life, as well as in business. It's best to prepare for it now.

* * * * * * * *

Jason Mangrum, Founder
http://www.BusinessEthicsFoundation.com
http://www.InsidetheMarketingMachine.com
http://www.AlmostSuperHuman.com
http://www.IncomeFL.com

Jason Mangrum is a 23-year-old internet marketing consultant, author, and spiritual practitioner. He is also the founder of the Business Ethics Foundation, as well as the co-creator of "Inside the Marketing Machine™ Newsletter, a weekly online publication dedicated to helping business owners and entrepreneurs realize the "marketing machine" within, and unlock their own human potential for unlimited success in business, and everyday life. Sign up for free by sending a blank email to: signupnow@insidethemarketingmachine.com or visit http://www.insidethemarketingmachine.com for more info…

A strong person and a waterfall always channel their own path - unknown

Eileen McCandless

Spiritual Hierarchy is neither a figment nor a product of man's imagination. It is an inner born belief and ideal where you set forth in motion a set of spiritual principled priorities. These spiritual principled priorities inadvertently become your own personal hierarchy towards becoming the best you can be.

You all possess them.

Spiritual hierarchy is simply an extension of your own personality. It is an adopted pattern of behavioural traits. It is an order of importance with how you yourself embrace your life. The spiritual hierarchy I practice comes packaged in the form of meditation.

My meditation teaches me: How to self-evaluate. How to Focus. How to relate to others. How to become compassionate and considerate towards others and me. How to walk my talk.

And more.

Each new day begins and ends with me in meditation. Although not so, it feels I have meditated since the moment I left my mother's womb. I don't recall, when, why or how I began my daily custom. It's a part of me, which I've never felt I need struggle against. The results of having regularly missed my daily practice reflects in my world as it slowly begins to unthread and fall apart. I learned from disciplined experience why my persistency and consistency in meditation works for me.

Does my meditation give me insightful information pertaining to me? Yes, absolutely. Do I pay close attention and act upon that which I should? No. Not always.

My meditation has taught me how my perceived perfection differs from another's perceived perfection. And truly at the end of the day – we are all perfect anyway. However, I make a concentrated effort to carry my inner strengths gained from meditation into all areas of my life. Including my work life. This I do in the form of energy.

Working with energy for me involves disciplined awareness, which is one way of measuring my own success. Success, for me, is knowing I have willingly and devotedly used my concentrated energy for the betterment of another. Each morning in meditation I prepare myself for what lies ahead of me throughout my day.

In raising my kundalini energy in meditation I am uniting myself with the supreme energy, which each and every one of us has complete access to. Becoming one with this supreme universal force allows me to enter into a clear frame of mind. It is this clear energy I carry into my work throughout my day. This clear energy helps me to assimilate and relate to others. This clear energy smoothes out any fears or misconceptions I may experience.

As my day begins in meditation, so it also ends in meditation. This is my time for introspection and reflection of my day's activities. Just how well did I comply with my own order of importance in my spiritual hierarchy? Do I need to make adjustments or perhaps modify my order of importance in the direction of my spiritual hierarchy? Was there a situation I could have handled better?

Each piece of work or situation I approach, I intentionally approach with love. I am so aware of how an "off" day for me can adversely effect the outcome for someone else who is depending on me or expects me to produce a fine work of art for them in the form of the written word.

On my "off" days, I am known to play music, yes even sing and dance. Meditate more. Look for humor. Or simply walk away from my task at hand. Then I begin again the next day with a positive outlook. Why? Well, its simple really.

When you attempt to produce a masterpiece for your customer or client while in a negative frame of mind - chances are all you will produce is failure. Yes, failure. You see everything, which you and I feel, touch, taste, hear, see and not see, is derived from energy. All energy is the heartbeat of existence. All energy beats at a different rate of vibration. Think of vibration as notes in of a music scale, how one note resonates higher than the next note. Where only the musician can capture their right note.

You and I are our own musicians in our own spiritual hierarchy. When my energy does not vibrate at my desired rate of vibration, then I take away from my finished outcome. And this I do not allow. I purposely enter into work with love, lightness and the longing to assist those who have come knocking at my door.

Let me explain.

Suppose I am one of many people working on a project. And just for supposing sake lets say a few people come into work Monday morning hung over, sick and or cranky. How do you suppose the outcome will turn out? You guessed it. Failure to a certain degree.

Can you think of the times in your own personal life or work life you have experienced a similar situation? Or perhaps when there were a bunch of you in a given situation all jockeying for control. Was there love in this scenario? Of course not. Was the energy pulsating through your body at that time focused towards your four elements of: customer – client – product – service? How could it be?

When you don't place your four elements at the center of your attention, when you are not on the same page, when you are not in the same loving frame of mind – would you not say you have begun to sabotage the final outcome long before the project has begun?

Imagine the positive effect of turning around and pouring this same energy into producing something far more constructive for another to benefit.

Take a gamble. Try it out sometime.

It only makes good sense how my altered state of thought process trained me how to look at and handle situations differently in my work life and personal life. For me it works. And it works well. Is my spiritual hierarchy unique? No, not at all. There are thousands upon thousands of people whom also carry their spiritual hierarchy into their work life and personal lives.

However, there are just not enough of us. Practicing it. Doing it. Accomplishing it.

At my current rate of vibration I listen as my inner voice says, "you've come along way babe, but you've still a long way to go". I guess in reality, you and I are still Gods in the making. Much like the flavor of the century, spiritual hierarchy changes as we all slowly evolve. It's nothing new. It's called growth. The rapport I laboriously establish with my inner voice leaves me feeling pretty confident we are all on track as a whole in our spiritual hierarchy.

And you?

What does your inner voice say?

Really, if you stop and think about it does the word "values" come to mind for you? Or perhaps otherwise known as the "golden rule" – do unto others! Because this is what "spiritual hierarchy" "meditation" and "golden rule" are all about. They are all about plain old common sense inner values. No revelation. No epiphany. They are all about becoming a creature of habit in the positive sense.

As realization surfaces and enlightens you it also informs you of; whatever you decide to approach in life, with the right energy, has a greater success rate towards its final outcome.

As the song sings, "all you need is love, love - love is all you need".

* * * * * * * *

Eileen Bernadette McCandless
Author: In the Presence of Grace
poet / writer / copywriter
http://www.copywriterqueen.com/
http://www.mccandlesscollection.com/
info@mccandlesscollection.com
mccandless@telus.net

"Aerodynamically the bumble bee shouldn't be able to fly, but the bumble bee doesn't know it so it goes on flying anyway."
~~Mary Kay Ash

Larry McLauchlin

1) New information reveals that 75%+ of the world's most successful people are profoundly spiritual in both belief and practice. Describe how your personal and business success has evolved through Spiritual Influences.

Several years ago, I went through a process that I call Spiritual Purpose. A Spiritual Purpose is only about you as spirit (Oneness) whereas what we normally call a life purpose is about what you are attempting to do in the world (duality).

The wonderful thing about discovering my Spiritual Purpose is that it now allows me to effortlessly determine whether what I am doing, what I am proposing to do or if any business opportunity that I am considering is truly aligned with my Spiritual Purpose. If it is - great! Lets do it! If it isn't - no thanks! Next?

In this way, I am able to instantly distinguish if any action, relationship, product, service, business opportunity, etc. is life expanding or life draining. In other words, my Spiritual Purpose allows me to see if a particular choice would in fact create stress, anxiety, worry, concern, duress, and problems because it is in some way counter to the Spiritual Purpose of my life. For example: there are many ways to quickly make large profits on the internet and since they are not aligned with my Spiritual Purpose I don't get involved with them. I know that such involvement would actually reverse my own spiritual growth.

Aligning with my spiritual values allows me to create and market products that allow my clients to grow spiritually, release their hidden potential, and live a full and complete life. Having a Spiritual Purpose allows me to live (BE) in poise and power.

2) In what ways do you incorporate your Spiritual Beliefs into day-to-day business interactions?

My daily activities are about DOING and as we are human beings and not human-doings – daily living is about BEING. It's about who or what I am. Naturally, who and what I am is evident in what I am doing. In fact, it's very obvious. For example: in my attitude. When I am living my spiritual values, I appear in the world as; integrity, love, kindness, respect, nurturing, creative, prosperous, compassionate and non-judgmental, to name just a few. The most amazing thing is that the people who are attracted to my businesses and me demonstrate the same love based behaviours in return.

3) What is the single-most important spiritual practice that promotes peace and prosperity within your own life?

By living life as LOVE, I can more easily experience everything in the world as ONE. When I began to experience everything external to me as being one with me - my life became calm, peaceful, and powerful. It's called poise.

To have poise means to live in that state of consciousness wherein peace and power thoroughly combine. The feeling of power becomes perfectly serene and the feeling of peace becomes enormously strong. When you feel absolutely calm and at the same time feel strong enough to move mountains, you are in POISE.

4) Imagine you are having a conversation with God (or the Universal creator or whatever name you prefer)... Share with us what is being said about the scope and future of Spirituality in the Entrepreneurial Business world.

The business world is gradually awakening to "living by the rule of love" and is letting go of "living by the rule of fear." Entrepreneurial businesses are leading the way. The entrepreneurial business owner, because he or she has greater control over everyday practices and activities, is becoming conspicuous because of both their spiritual and financial successes.

The successful entrepreneur does not compartmentalize their life into what he or she does when they are working and what they are doing when they are not working. Spirituality pervades their entire life.

Naturally, the actions and results of the spiritual entrepreneur will become more and more apparent to larger corporations. Corporations will observe how "spirituality at work" assists people to grow humanly and use more of their "God given" potential. Because of this they are creating greater success and satisfaction for both themselves and the company. Entrepreneurs and corporations alike will realize that spiritual beliefs and practices affect everyone including: clients, customers, suppliers, community, family, colleagues, and the environment

Even more entrepreneurs and corporations will begin to institute spirituality into their workplace, and not just as a management fad. These corporations will experience similar success to today's spiritually minded entrepreneur. The word spirituality will no longer elicit an embarrassing silence in corporate boardrooms.

The consciousness level of the entire world's population will continue to increase quickly and dramatically causing more and more of the "general population" to want to do more than just making a living. They will want a full and complete life living, as Spirit is the only solution.

* * * * * * * *

Larry McLauchlin
larry@ProsperitySecrets.com
ProsperitySecrets.com Inc.
3107 – 45 Street S.W.
Calgary AB Canada T3E 3T7

Visit http://www.ProsperitySecrets.com and purchase any ebook, email the proof of purchase to larry@ProsperitySecrets.com include the words Entrepreneurial Spirits in the subject line and I will personally email a free ebook - Mastery of Self – by Christian Larson – **a $24.95 value Free.**

"A great seer from India once said, 'You are where your attention takes you. In fact, you are your attention. If your attention is fragmented, you are fragmented. When your attention is in the past, you are in the past. When your attention is in the present moment, you are in the presence of God and God is present in you.'" - Deepak Chopra

---

Richard Monette

1) New information reveals that 75%+ of the world's most successful people are profoundly spiritual in both belief and practice. Describe how your personal and business success has evolved through Spiritual Influences.

My most profound belief is expressed in my book, The Gift - A story about finding a better score in golf and life, when the main character, Irving Pirsig Junior, describes one of the corner stones of his own successful pursuit of greatness when he states:

"Right or wrong, I had come to the conclusion that the search for greatness was either a spiritual process or nothing at all."

As Pirsig states, each and everyone of us are on a quest for achievement and performance, but this quest is futile if it doesn't lead to a higher sense of fulfillment as well. I realized early on in my career (and my life) that the quest for achievement is pretty straightforward: the more time and energy you invest, usually the more you achieve. The real challenge I have taken on is to also integrate a spiritual dimension to my quest. I believe my success is the outcome of my commitment to plan, decide and act in a spirit of helpfulness for all those involved.

I believe that my success to date is an outcome of connecting each and every of my decisions in the broader context of achieving good for all those involved.

2) In what ways do you incorporate your Spiritual Beliefs into day-to-day business interactions?

We live in a world of symbol. As human being we learn best through stories. From the beginning we decided to tell important stories to teach. In that perspective, I call mycorporate logo the InnerWarrior (see attachment) tells our story. This symbol represents the value-based commitment to plan, decide and act based on spiritual values.

"The Inner warrior is fighting against personal weaknesses and limitations against the forces that oppose the increase in knowledge and power. The InnerWarrior's fight is a struggle for harmony and freedom that begins inside and projects itself to the world of our actions. It is a quiet, unrelenting, and joyful QUESTS"

3) What is the single-most important spiritual practice that promotes peace and prosperity within your own life?

This is an interesting question, but for me I would have to say it is playing golf. I had quite a serious accident in the winter of 1993 in which I barely escaped death.

The following summer, recovering from two broken legs, I took up golf. I fell passionately in love with the game for one reason: it revealed my strengths and weaknesses of character.

Fundamentally, the person I used to be was not conducive to being a good golfer (too impatient, self-centered, cocky etc.). By facing these character traits through golf, I completed a personal self-transformation in which I discovered another side to myself, a side that is connected to the bigger picture. Every time I play golf, or walk in nature with my young children or visit a beautiful part of our world, I reconnect with the spiritual dimension of helpfulness for all.

4) Imagine you are having a conversation with God (or the Universal creator or whatever name you prefer). Share with us what is being said about the scope and future of Spirituality in the Entrepreneurial Business world.

This is simple. I believe our society is at a crossroad. In my daily work with corporate leaders, I realize that they are looking for improved performance, but that this quest must also make sense in a bigger frame corporate leaders are now also looking for a sense of fulfillment. Often, they are not quite sure what is missing, or they don't really know how to approach the topic, but they are looking for bigger answers. I believe the future scope of Spirituality in the Entrepreneurial Business World will be a quest for performance AND fulfillment at the strategic tactical AND personal levels.

* * * * * * * *

Richard Monette Bsc.Bed.M.A.
InnerWarrior Consulting
Phone: (403) 762 9192 / Toll free: (866) 762 9193
Web: http://www.InnerWarrior.com
Mail: Box 2028, Banff, Ab, T1L 1B8

"The world is for those who make their dreams come true." - Harold Gray

---

Lorrie Morgan-Ferrero

1) New information reveals that 75%+ of the world's most successful people are profoundly spiritual in both belief and practice. Describe how your personal and business success has evolved through Spiritual Influences.

It's very interesting how much my spirituality actually DOES affect my business every single day. I've always been an "independent creative". In other words, I enjoyed working by myself and doing things "my" way. In general I was happy being a freelance writer, an actress and a mom when I got out of college. Then when I had to support myself after my divorce, I had to make decisions based more on business and less on emotion. It was uncomfortable at first. I thought I was "selling out" and had to be ruthless. It took a little stretching that new business muscle to realize I didn't have to change my core beliefs to be successful. In fact, the more I went back to doing things the "natural" way for me, which involves listening to intuition and being grateful for what I have, the more business, joy and empowerment seem to come my way. I still run into people and situations I feel are not in integrity. But instead of taking them personally, I try to ask God to show me the bigger picture of what I need to know.

2) In what ways do you incorporate your Spiritual Beliefs into day-to-day business interactions?

Well, I do a lot more praying and acknowledging the gifts I have now. When things get me down (and they do) I try to turn to my higher power and ask what the lesson is in this event I'm supposed to get. It seems the more people know you, the more criticism you get. Sometimes I dread doing anything public because I know there will undoubtedly be some negative feedback. I don't know how celebrities handle it. I'm trying though. Trying not to let negativity bother me and ask what I need to know. I have to turn to God for help on this one often.

3) What is the single-most important spiritual practice that promotes peace and prosperity within your own life?

Helping others without anyone else knowing. It's easy to get caught up in everyday worries. But somehow when I help others and take the focus off of me, I feel more at ease, more useful.

4) Imagine you are having a conversation with God (or the Universal creator or whatever name you prefer)... Share with us what is being said about the scope and future of Spirituality in the Entrepreneurial Business world.

God rocks. God is so much easier on us than we are. I feel God is a joyful spirit and that's all He wants for us…joy, love and laughter. God really likes it when we laugh. You can feel His presence. Everything is perfect when you're aware of your God-self. Sadly that perfect feeling is fleeting. I always strive to keep close but it seems to be a process of forgetting and remembering.

* * * * * * * *

Lorrie Morgan-Ferrero
America's Copywriting Expert
http://www.red-hot-copy.com
http://www.copycampus.com

Destiny is not a matter of chance but of choice. Not something to wish for but to attain.- William Jennings Bryan

---

Herman Müller

1) New information reveals that 75%+ of the world's most successful people are profoundly spiritual in both belief and practice. Describe how your personal and business success has evolved through Spiritual Influences.

Spiritual Awareness and Success.

Successful people trust themselves and work with 'gut feelings' and intuition.
Self-trust is following the inner voice of 'the higher self consciousness' that directs our true purpose in earth. As we allow a free flow of our true potential there is no better guide on earth that our own soul for our 'sole purpose'. This gives us more opportunity to utilise the field of unlimited possibilities that we are all part of.

Spirituality is this inner creative force that radiates externally as enthusiasm and charisma. This unlimited energy of life itself, experienced and focussed into order, discipline and good management creates the core of all success.

This is my interpretation of Spirituality. I can attribute my success to this simple philosophy.

It is an evolving process of many stepping stones of life experiences that eventually mature into an awareness that seems allow me to flow with life.

2) In what ways do you incorporate your Spiritual Beliefs into day-to-day business interactions?

My enthusiasm and energy for my work and play has been maintained throughout my life as I kept my focus on this principle.

"Only change your work, profession or environment when you are happy and at the peak of success."

Firstly, this joy and success is the stepping-stone to a higher achievement. You take your self-confidence and experience with you to the next level. Use all your past experience as an education and training for what is to come. This is the essence of trust in yourself.

Secondly, you leave behind for others; something you have proven is good for them, as it was good for you. This is true spiritual service to you and equally to others.

Thirdly, the best decisions are made when happiness is indicating to you that there is harmony and balance in what you are doing. When you are not pleased or are unsuccessful, be aware there is something to learn that must be brought into the light for you to notice. A spiritual person cannot leave this for someone else when you know through your own experience what is not good for you. Make it good before passing it on, or the *'re- sent- ment'* will follow you until you; *'re-sent'* to see what *'was meant'* to be overcome. When you do this you will have *'en-lightenment'*. "

3) What is the single-most important spiritual practice that promotes peace and prosperity within your own life?

Compassion for yourself and others by accepting our human element of 'learning, and *'be-living'* this. "Do unto others as you wish others do unto you". This frees an enormous amount of energy and enthusiasm to be creative and find new and better ways for success.

4) Imagine you are having a conversation with God (or the Universal creator or whatever name you prefer)... Share with us what is being said about the scope and future of Spirituality in the Entrepreneurial Business world.

As I watch every bit of the news every day and share the worlds experiences and commentaries I pray,

"Oh God! I often see and feel your smile of infinite patience as you watch us struggle and fight each other to prove which is the 'right God', how we must follow 'your command' and how we are destroying this beautiful planet!

I realise that those who think and do this feel they must be greater than you and they are the ones that must show You their way!

Then I too smile; I send them the thoughts and a feeling of compassion that they may see the bigger picture and Your plan is well 'in hand'. Patience and learning will teach us all that we live at each moment of time, in a point of learning. I send them 'Your smile Your compassion and Your patience', that they may see the learning, trust themselves and allow others to be what they believe and be-and- live in what they themselves are!"

* * * * * * * *

Herman Müller
email; hermannmuller@earthlink,net
harmony@qldnet.com.au
websites :- http://www.harmony.au.com/
http://www.the-profiler.net/

Author of "Face to Face with Facts" and "Guidance from The Masters"

Director/Founder of The Australasian Institute of Body-Mind Analysis and Psychosomatic Therapy. This a Registered Training Organisation providing a "Diploma in Psychosomatic Therapy"

This is a 'National Recognised Training'. This training by me was commenced and expanded since 1993 in Australia, North America. Europe and New Zealand and developed to a Teacher's Training Diploma Level.

I have a background as Sports trainer, 25 years in the management field, lecturing internationally, a Psychosomatic Therapist, Master Practitioner in Hypnotherapy, Neurolinguistic Programming and Time Line Therapy, a Teacher of Esoteric Science, Emotional Release Bodywork, trainer for Meditation and a student of many religions, Ayurvedic and Tantric Sciences. Born in India in 1936 of German grand parents I have settled in Australia since 1967. I have been travelling Internationally for the past 14 years as a trainer and light net-worker.

"The universe never says no to your thought about yourself. It only grows it." -- Neale Donald Walsch

---

Jo Han Mok

1) New information reveals that 75%+ of the world's most successful people are profoundly spiritual in both belief and practice. Describe how your personal and business success has evolved through Spiritual Influences.

I think business without spirituality is like having a hamburger without a beef patty. I echo the opinion of people like Bruce Barton and Joe Vitale, that business is really hands down the best teacher of life, primarily because of the challenges that are pushed in your way.

You need to be an, 'over-comer' to succeed in business. You need to summon strength that you ordinarily would not have from WITHIN to deal with the hurdles and obstacles that come your way, and if that is not spiritual, I don't know what is.

I wasn't born with a silver spoon in my mouth. I didn't have it that difficult, but I didn't have it that easy either.

I built my business from scratch, and here's the 'spiritual process' that I used.

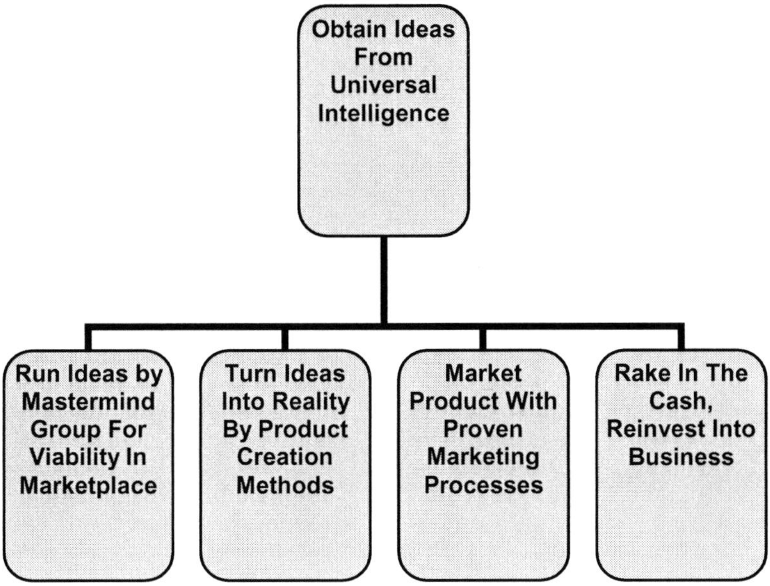

Jo Han Mok's Spiritual Wealth Creation Process

As you can see, the entire wealth creation process begins internally. I claim absolutely no originality to this entire process but I am pretty positive most internal 'wealth creation' processes bear some similarity to this model.

Personally, I am of the opinion that what we term the 'subconscious' is actually the link between the physical and that of the realm of the unseen.

I cannot prove it with empirical evidence, but I can share my experience in how tapping into this realm can bring about pretty astounding results.

Here's what I usually do.

I feed my subconscious mind data from my conscious mind. These are usually intentions that I set, and goals that I want to accomplish. Using Psycho Cybernetic techniques, I can usually see the 'end results' crystal clearly and so tangibly that I can almost 'touch and feel it'.

And as a result, the subconscious mind cannot differentiate between fiction and reality and the lines become blurred.

Then I simply start 'faking' it until I make it.

Here are some of the results I obtained using this process:

- I started a six figure income business part time from a tiny apartment in Boston where I was struggling as a full time college student.

- I've forged strategic host beneficiary relationships with people I only DREAMT of working with. People like Jeff Paul, Joe Vitale, Ted Ciuba, etc.

- I've shared the speaking platform with luminaries like Armand Morin, Randy Charach, Frank Garon and Peter Sun, etc. People whom I used to bow to when I was a rookie. This is in spite of people perceiving me as a guy with an incomprehensible accent. Still I've made 5 figures in one hour from speaking, so that's not much of deterrence.

- I now run my own marketing company, Midas Touch Marketing with three staff and together with my partner Ewen Chia, own real estate and live in a beautiful condo in prime area when people my age in Singapore see making $3k a month a challenge and mostly live with their parents.

- I routinely get paid as much as $25k to write a sales letter. Needless to say, it makes me even happier when the sales letters I've written for my clients have pulled in hundreds and thousands of dollars.

- I'm also the Director of Web Analytics in the biggest Web Analytics company in Asia.

And I'm not listing these achievements to pat myself on the back. I'm telling you all this that this process works, and if someone like me can make it work, there really isn't' any conceivable reason why you cannot make it work too.

More importantly, I'd like to quote Jim Rohn, "Its not that becoming an millionaire is important. It's what you become in the process of becoming a millionaire"

2) In what ways do you incorporate your Spiritual Beliefs into day-to-day business interactions?

I believe in that whatever you give more of, you get more of. In my business interactions, I seek to give as much as possible, knowing it will come back to me, multiplied, ten, hundredfold? This is also why; I do not hesitate to unconditionally share some of the best knowledge I've acquired with people on my list. Because the more value I give to them, the more they give to me, in terms of loyalty, spiritual fulfillment and of course money when they buy my products.

3) What is the single-most important spiritual practice that promotes peace and prosperity within your own life?

Actually, there are two; yoga and music. For me, yoga has demonstrated what the term 'breath of life' truly means, and the benefits of doing yoga are way too many to list here, suffice to say, there are spiritual, physical and physiological benefits. Music, especially jazz, is like a conduit to the 'creative genius', which I practice regularly. (I'm a pianist).

One of my favorite quotes is "God gave us music so that we can pray without words"

4) Imagine you are having a conversation with God (or the Universal creator or whatever name you prefer)... Share with us what is being said about the scope and future of Spirituality in the Entrepreneurial Business world.

I think God would say something along the lines of "I gave the world business so that mankind would learn how to multiply his talents. To the entrepreneur, I would say, 'well done, good and faithful servant!"

* * * * * * * *

Jo Han Mok is a frequent guest and featured speaker at Internet Marketing bootcamps and conferences on subjects such as copywriting and Joint Venture Marketing. Visit his website: to get a simple step-by-step plan that can take you from ground zero to having money deposited in your bank account from an online business every single day for the rest of your life!

http://www.SuperFastProfit.com

"To attract attractive people, you must be attractive. To attract powerful people, you must be powerful. To attract committed people, you must be committed. Instead of going to work on them, you go to work on yourself. If you become, you can attract."
--Jim Rohn

Ted Nicholas

1) New information reveals that 75%+ of the worlds most successful people are profoundly spiritual in both belief and practice. Describe how your personal and business success has evolved through Spiritual Influences.

I've evolved from devout Christian (Greek Orthodox). But I questioned my early religious teachings. I was dissatisfied with the answers by religious leaders and in every book I could read on the topic.

My doubts led to agnosticism.

Upon discovering the work of author Ayn Rand, especially her book "Atlas Shrugged", I became an atheist. I consider the late Miss Rand the best mind of the 20th century.

But even though I would debate anyone about it, deep down I was not completely comfortable with my atheistic, albeit objective and rational view of the universe. Intellectually it just didn't feel right. There had to be more. And I discovered there is.

Today I consider myself a completely spiritual individual. And I've never been happier.

To my "higher power" I pray every day about the important aspects of my life. Health, family, clients, fellow humans, business outcomes are all subjects of my meditation and prayers.

I can say without exception every single prayer during my entire life has been favorably answered.

Since adopting my present philosophy, my personal and business success has dramatically improved. And this success seems to expand geometrically.

Finally, a word about organized religion.

The best thing about it is having a set of values. This, of course, everyone needs. So it is a real benefit and comfort for many.

However, for the most part I feel religion is extremely harmful.

In human history an estimated 100,000,000 (that's million!) people have been slaughtered in the name of religion. No other factor comes even close. Much of the mass murder is due to some religious group waiting to impose their views by force upon others. I can think of no greater crime.

As any serious student of history knows, every religious belief system, whether Christian, Jew, Buddhist, Muslim, etc., all rest on a fallacy.

Each religion believes there is but one true God.

This is not only erroneous. It's patently absurd. Clearly this cannot be.

I submit there is a higher power, a supreme being, a "God" if you like. I believe this "God" operates both outside of us and within our very spirit and soul. It is the most powerful force in the universe.

I cannot prove this point. It does require a leap of faith. But my empirical experience in life has convinced me of its truth.

2) What is the single-most important spiritual practice that promotes peace and prosperity within your own life?

Prior to making any important decision, or having a major business meeting, or launching a major product or marketing campaign, I pray for the result I want and feel I truly deserve.

3) What is the single-most important spiritual practice that promotes peace and prosperity within your own life?

Keeping a daily personal journal. First, I basically enter a state of daily appreciation for all the emotional, physical and natural blessings, which I've been provided.

Then I answer two basic questions:

(1) What am I presently feeling?
(2) What do I want?

This helps to keep me in touch with my inner self.

4) Imagine you are having a conversation with God (or the Universal creator or whatever name you prefer)- Share with us what is being said about the scope and future of Spirituality in the Entrepreneurial Business world.

Dear "Higher Power,"

First, I want you to know how much I appreciate you and all you've done for me. As a token of my appreciation, I'm trying to do all in my power to help my fellow humans. But, I'm sure I could do more. I want you to lead me toward new directions where I could be of more service.

Please help me find better ways to communicate to all entrepreneurs that they are the real undiscovered heroes of this universe.

Entrepreneurs are the creators of all communication breakthroughs, all jobs, all trade, all wealth, all human freedom and all that is good. But more entrepreneurs need to grasp and recognize this truth, as so few really do. I need your guidance on a daily basis. I am honored to be your messenger and servant.

* * * * * * * *

To get complete information on Ted Nicholas products and services,as well as subscribe to Ted's free e-zine, *The Success Margin*, go to:http://www.tednicholas.com/

"Leap, and the net appears." - Julia Cameron

Pat O'Bryan

1) Describe how your personal and business success has evolved through Spiritual Influences.

My spiritual practice is a combination of Zen and Tao, with a focus on choosing the right path and following it, without getting caught up in the minutia. It's all about alignment, isn't it?

If you're on the right path, you'll get where you want to go. Of course, you need to pick your destination carefully. Through meditation and journaling, I've explored my core beliefs. Sometimes what you think isn't what you believe, this takes some time. When I'm choosing an intention, I examine it closely to make sure it's in alignment with my beliefs. For example, I never do anything just for money. I'm very interested in money, but for an intention to work for me, it's important that it couples profit with "good work."

Good work is a concept I picked up from E.F. Schumacher's book of the same name, back in my college days. It rang true to me then, and it still does.

Once you've picked your destination and committed yourself to the right path, the trick and this is the absolute key to the whole philosophy is to enjoy the scenery, and not worry about getting to the destination. Just let go. The path doesn't lead anywhere but where you want to go.

I haven't analyzed it very much, but I suspect there's some solid science behind this. Having set my intention to accomplish a certain goal, I'm in total alignment with this intention. My facial expressions, body language, choice of words and inflection; my whole conscious and subconscious presentation to the world, is in alignment with my intention.

That's a tremendous advantage, it's my suspicion that a lot of people are chasing dreams that aren't really their dreams, and trying to achieve goals that aren't really their goals. I can empathize, I did that for years. It's impossible to focus your energy under those conditions.

The evolution of my personal and business successes came together when Dr. Joe Vitale handed me a copy of his book, "Spiritual Marketing." I had everything I needed in terms of skill and knowledge, from years of education and practice. I had a strong foundation in spirituality, from reading Alan Watts, Thich Nhat Han, Alan Ginsberg, and other writers whose work resonated in me. It wasn't until I read "Spiritual Marketing" that it all came together, and I understood how important it was to align my commercial adventures with my spiritual practice.

It's been about a year since I first read that book. In that time, my income has increased by an order of magnitude, but that's just a side effect. The real benefit to me is that I spend every minute of my life doing exactly what I want to do. Because I'm on the right path, everything I do is taking me another step down that path towards my goals.

2) In what ways do you incorporate your Spiritual Beliefs into day-to-day business interactions?

I enter each interaction mindful of my intention and don't get attached to the outcome. The non-attachment is the tricky part. I do the next right thing.

When it comes to the day-to-day work I do, writing, designing products, composing and recording music, writing sales letters and designing web sites, I set the intention and then let go. The universe provides whatever I need whether it's the next chapter, or an interesting chord progression, or a graphic design. The times when I've tried to force these things out of myself have been painfully frustrating. When I let go and trust the path to lead me to the next stop on my journey, the work is done effortlessly. I like effortlessly.

3) What is the single-most important spiritual practice that promotes peace and prosperity within your own life?

Meditation is the first step. I think of it as "re-booting." Starting the day with a clear and focused mind makes each day more productive and keeps me focused on doing the next right thing. Another practice that I consider spiritual is writing. I keep a journal, and use that as a place to let my mind tell me what it's thinking. I find that the act of writing is useful to help me focus. I credit Julia Cameron, whose books I treasure and re-read constantly, with being the writer who first revealed this secret to me. I would never start a project or set an intention without first journaling it.

4) Imagine you are having a conversation with God (or the Universal creator or whatever name you prefer)... Share with us what is being said about the scope and future of Spirituality in the Entrepreneurial Business world.

Answer #1 I'm not sure there's any connection between spirituality and the concept of "God." If there is a universal creator, they're ignoring some issues that are a lot more important to me than the "entrepreneurial business world." I'd try to point this out.

Answer #2 My conversation with God:

Me, "Thank you."

God, "No problem. Now go play."

* * * * * * * *

Pat O'Bryan is the Director of the Milagro Research Institute. You can find links to his many projects at http://www.patobryan.com. He is the publisher of two ezines: Milagro World (http://www.milagroworld.com) and Effortless E-Books (http://www.EffortlessEbooks.com). He is also a recording artist who tours Europe with his band several times a year. He lives in the Texas Hill Country with his partner and their three children.

"The moment of enlightenment is when a person's dreams of possibilities become images of probabilities." - Vic Braden

---

Alan Ogden

Hollywood Birth's the Anti-Prosperity Movement

Well, who else would do it?

Before I became convinced of the whole possibility of spirit involvement in my life, I was studying the underlying trends that affect the way people live in North America.

I discovered that the United States of America was founded on the principles of the Bible. Not preaching or the idea of religion, but a spirit based idea surrounding the pursuit of our life's enjoyment. It affected every aspect of life and still does to this day. Our country (Canada) and the US were to be a haven for people to reach the absolute height of their potential.

So, what happened?

We invented entertainment! Radio, Television and other forms of entertainment where every principle we have lived by could be dissected, questioned, criticized and eventually challenged to the point where mediocrity and subversion became the norm. You believe what? Let's create a television special to embarrass you.

People of spiritual enlightenment headed underground and fast. No one wanted to even let on they believed in something. No one wanted to even talk about it, write about it or publicly admit. Soon the only visible were the "weird" or "weak".

As I continued to look and ponder this, an amazing realization struck me. "Thoughts become things". That's right. Thoughts, the ultimate form of energy, were actually manifesting themselves as reality. Now, I know many will argue, but if you think about it, either your own thoughts or the thoughts of others, that you accept, become what we experience.

The problem, of course, is so many do not think for themselves and therefore the mass consciousness is what they experience and they believe life is outside of their control.

Well, when I really began to understand this concept, I was ready for some deeper study. I discovered that every time I took the control over my thoughts, expressed them through writing or recording, and focused on the outcome, the people and events “materialized”. I now understand everyone has experienced this.

Think about your present partner in life, if you are enjoying one. Did you not first think about it, then focus on it and what happened? The events, often called coincidence, occurred. Sometimes these events happen so quickly after we have thought about the outcome we desire, we are shocked into questioning; “is there a greater force at work here?” Of course, no one takes this too seriously because we wouldn’t want to let something out of our control effect us.

All this lead me wondering, and now I believe there is a great benefit from harnessing our thoughts, making intentional decisions and focusing in this way. I discovered, as well, many others were coming to this conclusion at the same time and, amazingly, we seemed to be “finding” one another. I now not only believe in higher powers, I employ them in my life.

The decision to employ these did not come easy. My logical mind doesn’t want to give up easily, often wanting to think things out and feeling like it should know all the answers. In spite of this, I decided to go ahead and just accept the facts.

Now I find the best single practice I can employ, is to think about the OUTCOME I am after. I then write a letter to myself, or someone important to me AS IF the events have already occurred. I often make fun of the struggles and explaining how easy it all really was. I then file the letter away or keep it handy for daily reading if I am really struggling with the belief the events will occur, just as I stated.

Once I have written the letter, I remain open to any and all possibilities. Sometimes things will happen that appear negative to the outcome, but my experience has taught me sometimes things are not as they appear and I can safely trust the process. I find this step to be the most difficult.

We are not a society that likes to wait.

When I feel anxious, I sit in a quiet place and have a conversation with the universe or God. I read my letter and just ask for the understanding and patience to see it all through. I find that when I do this, a peace either comes or an insight that helps me to adjust my outcome.

When this happens I simply rewrite the letter stating what happened and reaffirming the outcome. It is all very simple. There is no mantras, singing or humming. I find it to be really quite logical, a pre-determination if you will. I can have many outcomes in different areas at the same time, but I do write different letters for each.

My sincere hope is this information will help some one else. I don't think of it as weird or necessarily spiritual in a religious sense. I often talk about it to others. It is always amazing to watch as they to realize; "you know I have had things happen like that" and understand it can be this way all the time.

Do my outcomes always manifest?

Yes, as long as they do not provide for hurt or loss to another. This is my rule. I know that others will intentionally direct their thoughts to the hurt of another, but I have chosen a different path. This is because I am convinced there is enough of everything good for all. It is just waiting to manifest for the thinker.

Happy thinking. And remember; thoughts become things. Choose good ones.

* * * * * * * *

Alan Ogden
Calgary, AB
Sept/19/04

Deep within man dwell those slumbering powers; powers that would astonish him, that he never dreamed of possessing; forces that would revolutionize his life if aroused and put into action. - Orison Swett Marden

---

PerfectCustomers, Inc.

(Jan Stringer, Stacey Hall, Alan Hickman)

1) New information reveals that 75%+ of the world's most successful people are profoundly spiritual in both belief and practice. Describe how your personal and business success has evolved through Spiritual Influences.

The triad of our business partnership, Jan – Stacey – Alan, came to together out of the very nature of our work based on the Universal Law of Attraction. In our book, "Attracting Perfect Customers…. The Power of Strategic Synchronicity" we share our unique Strategic Attraction Planning Process™ that asks the reader to consider four questions that are applicable to all types of relationships – business and personal:

1. What are the Qualities, Characteristics, Attributes of your Perfect Customer?
2. What makes them (my Perfect Customer) and / or me tick?
3. What do I want my Perfect Customers, to expect of me?
4. What is there to improve to become more attractive?

The second question delves into the heart and soul as reflected back to us by our Perfect Customers (i.e. Perfect refers to someone who is a perfect "fit" for us). We have found that most relationships overlook this question when considering whether they want to do business with someone, however, in our company we believe that the answer to this question is perhaps the most important question to ask.

PerfectCustomers, Inc. believes that our business, and the businesses of tens of thousands of others world wide, has become successful as a result of our practice of strategically looking inward and towards our connection to God.

2) In what ways do you incorporate your Spiritual Beliefs into day-to-day business interactions?

Our day-to-day business interactions are the same whether we are in a business or personal setting. To us there is no difference in how we "talk" whether we are with a client or a personal friend. To us we build all of our relationships using the same principles that we teach, in other words, we "walk our talk".

Everything we teach is based on Spiritual principles that can be found in the Ancient Wisdom of great teachings.

We use visualization as a way to center within and as a way to connect within first before taking any other actions. A typical class with us always starts with a "Centering" visualization session. In our classes and retreats, we speak openly about spirituality, God and Universal Truths. We stay open in our conversations to allow for all spiritual practices and beliefs so that any person can benefit from our teachings regardless of their unique beliefs.

3) What is the single-most important spiritual practice that promotes peace and prosperity within your own life?

In addition to our regular practice of the Strategic Attraction Planning Process™, each of us has our own spiritual practice: Alan, for example, has a daily practice of Meditation. Jan dances using the NIA technique, a body, mind and soul dance where she has found that she connects to God most through dance and nature. Stacey connects to God through Daily Prayer and Meditation.

4) Imagine you are having a conversation with God (or the Universal creator or whatever name you prefer). Share with us what is being said about the scope and future of Spirituality in the Entrepreneurial Business world.

- God says to each individual that the way to bring Spirituality into the Entrepreneurial Business world is by living true to one's purpose AT WORK.

- God says that the expression of the Divine Feminine must be expressed more fully in the work world through the honoring of intuition, and creativity with more emphasis on activities that allow the full free flow of the feminine energy.

- God says that people must be paid for who they are being in the world, rather than for what they do.

In the business place, it is now widely accepted that "Perfect Love" is the heart of every business and people are being taught in the workplace how to have intimate relationships.

* * * * * * * *

PerfectCustomers, Inc.
Jan Stringer, Stacey Hall, Alan Hickman
910 W. 14th – Houston, TX 77008
http://www.perfectcustomers.com

All is a miracle. The order of nature, the revolution of a hundred million of worlds around a million suns, the activity of light, the life of animals, all are grand and perpetual miracles.~ Voltaire

---

Lori Prokop

1) New information reveals that 75%+ of the world's most successful people are profoundly spiritual in both belief and practice. Describe how your personal and business success has evolved through Spiritual Influences.

It is important to have an inner foundation of peace. The outside world will reflect what is going on inside. When I meet people in turmoil, I realize what I see happening on the outside is a reflection of their inner beliefs. Parents and authority-figures give many of these beliefs. Parental and authority-figure beliefs do not just leave your mind as you grow from child to adult. To create the life outcomes you desire, you must realize these beliefs exist, identify them and replace them with current, relevant and healthy beliefs.

2) In what ways do you incorporate your Spiritual Beliefs into day-to-day business interactions?

One of our life purposes is to each be an "Earth Angel". What does this mean? It means to realize that your non-material higher power (God, Buddha or whomever) is able to radiate energy through physical bodies. The catch is, this higher power doesn't have a physical body. But you do. And that's where higher power, physical body and free will come together. You have the choice of what type of energy you would like to radiate to other humans. What choices are you making? Who are you?

What does it mean to ask the question, "Who are you?" And what kind of an answer are we looking for? It depends on the person asking. I'm asking you from a spiritual aspect. Who are you, when it comes to your energy, your vibration, your beliefs?"

I'm not talking about, do you have enough energy to work all day, pick up the kids, make dinner and mow the lawn. The energy I'm asking about is who are you while you are carrying out your daily tasks.

Your ability to find the inner peace that is already within you is very important right now. Don't wait for "enlightenment" or some sort of salvation before you choose your energy, your being and who you are.

3) What is the single-most important spiritual practice that promotes peace and prosperity within your own life?

Conscious living meanings looking at every step, action, thought and use of energy and asking, "What does this create?"

In this, you must decide what it is you want to create. My desire is peace, harmony, love, freedom, joy and abundance. Another desire is to walk the earth without judgment, guilt, blame or shame of others or myself.

When I measure my every step, action, thought and use of energy against these self-chosen guidelines, I have a spiritual practice, which promotes peace and prosperity.

4) Imagine you are having a conversation with God (or the Universal creator or whatever name you prefer)... Share with us what is being said about the scope and future of Spirituality in the Entrepreneurial Business world.

Many people desire to be spiritual beings. To do so, we have to take a look at how we live our time in these bodies. It is easy to be spiritual when one is sleeping. It is also acceptable and easier to be spiritual with your family. But when it comes to work, many people believe they must leave their spirituality at the door. How do they do this? By choosing fear over live.

Spirituality is not a religion. It is choosing love over fear.

It may appear that spirituality will not fare well in business. Some view spiritual beings as weak or soft. Just the opposite is true. While fear and competition may appear to force fast solutions, love creates solutions with lasting, positive results. The leaders of the future will be those with the ability to create business solutions from spirituality and love.

Lori Prokop, Best Selling Author and Speaker. To contact Lori email lori@bestsellerpublishing.com

* * * * * * * *

Lori Prokop

Senior Group Publisher, Best Seller Publishing, Inc.

676A Ninth Avenue #215
New York, New York 10036
800-521-5354
lori@bestsellerpublishing.com

Dreams are renewable. No matter what our age or condition, there are still untapped possibilities within us and new beauty waiting to be born. - Dr. Dale Turner

---

Leon Rawitz

Coincidences are Just God's Way of Acting Anonymously

It was out of the question. My friend Phil knew as much. Despite our "friendly" speech competitions in Toastmasters and our joint passions for pursuing professional speaking careers, were I to invest in another costly workshop, I would most certainly need to find a good divorce attorney. My understanding wife's patience had been fully tested. With each seminar I attended came the promise of a changed life,a promise that to date had been unrealized. And considering that I had just spent thousands of dollars with a speaking coach just months earlier, focusing on how to identify and uniquely position myself as a speaker, I didn't dare consider attending the Bill Gove "Weekend Speech Workshop".

It didn't matter how many giants from the speaking profession graduated from Bill's classor how many credited Bill Gove as being the single biggest influence in their speaking careers. It didn't even matter that my idol, the late Og Mandino, one of the most admired and respected inspirational authors and speakers of the 20th century was a graduate of the Bill Gove Speech Workshop. Nor could I let Bill's advancing years (he was a healthy 88 years old at the time) and the fear that if his health failed, this might be the last time to work with this speaking legend, influence my decision. The fact was, I had spent too much money already, and did not have the funds for yet another seminar.

Phil knew this, which is why he never asked me to attend. But he did cleverly ask for a "favor". Since he respected my opinion, would I mind inquiring about the workshop and then sharing my thoughts, even though he had already registered? I agreed.

I called and spoke to Bill's young partner, Steve Siebold, Bill's junior by nearly half a century. I told Steve that I had heard about the workshop and wanted to know more. As Steve described the syllabus for the weekend, I found myself silently acknowledging all the benefits. Whereas my most recent speech coaching was dedicated to identifying the topic, the contents and the target market for my speeches, this workshop was devoted entirely to delivering an effective speech through improved platform skills. It was the perfect complement to my prior training.

As Steve completed his description, he uttered six words that would change the course of my life, "And we have one seat left". Without a second's hesitation I said, "Count me in".

Normally, I agonize over most decisions. Not this time. Something inside told me that this was exactly what I needed to doand where I was supposed to be. But that didn't stop me from wondering to myself how in the world I was ever going to explain this to my wife.

Since the workshop was a little less than four weeks out, I decided that time was on my side. So I did what most brave husbands would have done, I didn't say anything. I needed time to plot my strategy. And that's when fate intervened.

The phone call from the College Park, Maryland based advertising agency, took me by surprise. For years, the agency owner had been pursuing us as a potential client. We were one of the biggest advertisers in our industry. But this time, his call was of a different nature. His agency was asked to present their capabilities and recommend strategies to a manufacturer who was steadily losing market share to "copycat" competitors. To prepare a speculative "pitch", he needed an industry insider who was familiar with exclusive distribution and could help formulate a strategic plan. Would I be interested in consulting with his company on this special project?

My answer was an emphatic "yes". The project was a fun one. For the first time in my marketing career, I got to sit on the advertising agency side of the business, rather than the client side. I began to appreciate just how much time and preparation goes into developing ideas, strategies, advertisements, and proposals for prospective clients. As I later learned from the agency owner, they stood a 1 in 4 chance of capturing this business. Two other advertising firms were also "bidding" for the account, as was their current advertising agency, a company that had held the business for the past three years.

For three weeks, I worked non-stop in evenings and weekends, "mystery shopping" the manufacturer's customers, gathering competitive intelligence, interviewing consumers, evaluating price points, merchandising, and developing various advertising themes, layouts, copy, and creating a new company positioning. As the various components of the campaign came together, we grew more and more excited about our recommendations and the prospects of "winning" this new business.

I did not attend the agency's presentation to the prospective client as I was gainfully employed elsewhere (I received prior permission from my employer to consult on this project during my off hours). However, the agency owner was very excited about the response he received from the company's principals. They appeared to fully embrace the ideas and directions that we had proposed. Now came the waiting part, did we or didn't we win the business?

The Bill Gove Speech Workshop was everything I could have ever hoped for. The Weekend was truly life changing. I thrived in such a supportive environment, surrounded by like-minded peers that had the same passion for delivering their heart-felt messages to the world as I did.

I learned from two masters in Bill and Steve, things that books and Toastmasters simply can't teach you, like how to craft a powerful speech by making points and telling stories, why pros like Bill and Steve always memorize their speeches, how to "lighten up" and not be too perfect (which makes you more real to your audience), great sources for finding humor and adding it to your talks, and how to be totally prepared and not panic in the event that you are asked to cut the length of your speech at the last minute (because a program is running over-schedule). And much, much more.

Each mini-speech that we gave during the weekend was recorded and evaluated first by Bill and Steve, and then by the attendees of the workshop. This was one of the most valuable parts of the entire weekend, speech critiques by the "master" himself who has accomplished everything there is to achieve in the speaking profession.

But let me share the most valuable lesson I learned this glorious weekend. It had absolutely nothing to do with public speaking. It was a lesson in life, compassion and understanding. Allow me to explain. One of the attendees in our workshop class was a very distinguished, middle-aged woman. She was a Psychologist and noted author. She appeared very "stand-offish", unlike everyone else in the class. I reasoned that she was very impressed with herself and her credentials, perhaps a little too impressed. Her speech evaluations of her fellow classmates were harsher than most. But as the weekend progressed, her guard began to lower and this incredible human being emerged. And then she shared a speech that affected me in a way that I have never been impacted before. It was the story of her oldest son. He was attending college in Washington, D.C. It was obvious from how she spoke of him that they shared a special bond and a love that appeared to have no bounds.

One morning, she received a call from the university, asking if she had heard from her son. His roommate and professors had not seen him the previous day and that was most unusual. He was a very studios and conscientious young man. She explained that she had spoken to him just two evenings before. He was happy and enjoying school. That was the last conversation they had together.

She immediately flew to Washington with her husband to accompany police and volunteers from the community and the university on a search. There was no trace of her son. Police were stumped, his fellow students in shock, and his family devastated. The grief and years of anguish from this seven year unsolved mystery had broken her heart,a heart that was now fully exposed in all of its pain and vulnerability before her audience. There was not a dry eye in the group.

In the span of 2 ½ days, my first impressions of a self-absorbed, egotistical psychologist and author had been transformed into one of the strongest, most courageous mothers, spouses, psychologists and fellow speakers I had ever met. I think it was Zig Ziglar that once said, treat every person you meet as if they were experiencing tremendous sorrow and you will most always be right.

The advertising agency that I consulted for did not "win" the new business. Unfortunately, the prospective client decided to stay with their incumbent firm (the company's revenue decline continued and they have since sold the business). However, the payment for my consulting fees was within $5.00 of the cost of the entire Bill Gove weekend workshop. And since that time, I had recouped my investment at least thirty-fold as evidenced by rapid career acceleration in the corporate world and now in private practice, all because of my ability to confidently and very competently speak in public. And yes, my dreams of speaking professionally have been realized.

Coincidence? I don't think so. This is what I was meant to do. Coincidences are just God's way of acting anonymously.

* * * * * * * *

Leon Rawitz
Fail Proof Marketing
http://www.failproofmarketing.com

"The ultimate value of life depends upon awareness and the power of contemplation rather than upon mere survival." -- Aristotle

---

John Robson

1. Describe how your personal and business success has evolved through Spiritual Influences.

I find spiritual influences work best where we have major deep seated NEEDS in our life, not WANTS and desires. I meditated on and wrote about seventy items to characterize my ideal relationship and met my wife who has them all. I idealized my perfect self employment with residual earning, much freedom, little stress, work at home, touching many lives deeply and that both my wife and I could do with little effort, yet lots of impact on the consciousness of humanity. We are living that life now.

I had been programming for a very nice house with lots of sunlight, nice office, next to nature, with our own garden and lots of places to enjoy reading and creative sessions with a view of nature. As a bonus, a nice car, and many extras also came into our life. It happened totally unexpectedly, with no mortgage or extra costs.

Our life flows with no major incidents. Life has been very good to us.

2) In what ways do you incorporate your Spiritual Beliefs into day-to-day business interactions?

The key for me is just **being conscious, paying attention, being in the present moment.** Too often I am into new things, trying to control my great life. And then I realize life does not work like that.

The key for me is **making and then taking time** to have my own sacred, silent, creative space ,at least one hour per day. I do different types of journaling. It is my main process to work with my creativity, inner guidance and synthesizing mind. I connect with my higher purpose, the tensions and issues in my life today and any new urges, ideas or potentials that I sense are unfolding. I track very closely the cycles I go through, cycles that affect my personality and cycles that stimulate and integrate my soul nature.

I often connect with the aspects of my purpose and essence and I ask lots of questions. E.g. How can I express my purpose today? How can I serve more people more deeply?

Then I jump into the day. I am sensitive to whether I do creative, inner work, or mundane maintenance and operations work. There needs to be a balance of this initiating and completing energy.

Rituals are important to me also. They are one of the most powerful ways to connect with my inner being and the power of my subconscious mind. So I create different metaphors to anchor key energies each day. I have a small bonsai garden that is very beautiful and as I nurture it and spray the moss many times per day, I visualize, use my imagination and sense how we nurture many people with our internet business.

3) What is the single-most important spiritual practice that promotes peace and prosperity within your own life?

In many years of trying to find the most important practice I have come to a conclusion, that there is no one practice that can create enough tension and integration to provide insights and consciousness change. It is an accumulation of much inner work that creates tension and transformational shifts. My belief is that one requires about four practices to shift a paradigm and consciousness. Pick the ones that work best for you but four practices can create enough tension from different perspectives that a holistic, holographic change takes place. I normally include and meditation, ritual, divination processes and journaling (often spiritual dialogue) and loving selfless service.

4) Imagine you having a conversation with God (or the Universal creator or whatever name you prefer) - Share with us what is being said about the scope and future of Spirituality in the Entrepreneurial Business world.

Our most untapped resource in humanity is the use of imagination. Without imagination one cannot love, create, be creative, live one's purpose or be intuitive. Our most untapped discipline is to be conscious, to be soul aware in all encounters and activities and perceiving. There is purpose and meaning to all we encounter, one only has to PAY ATTENTION to every sacred moment and to learn to let go, follow your imagination and guidance.

5) What hasn't been asked that should have been addressed or answered?

Yes, a key question.

What still blocks you from being the spiritual being you desire?

My need to be in the know, to understand and be in control. I do not let myself go. It is probably a fear of the unknown of being God-like and 100% responsible for all I could do. There is a need to tame the spiritual pride.

* * * * * * * *

John Robson
http://www.higherawareness.com

"Your profession is not what brings home your paycheck. Your profession is what you were put on earth to do with such passion and such intensity that it becomes spiritual in calling."
--Vincent Van Gogh

Sam Rosen

1) New information reveals that 75%+ of the world's most successful people are profoundly spiritual in both belief and practice. Describe how your personal and business success has evolved through Spiritual Influences.

The more spiritual I become, the more "spirituality" becomes an amorphous and complex idea to me.

When I first began my spiritual journey – if that is what you want to call it – success was the last topic on my mind. I had been diagnosed with Attention Deficit Disorder in my early youth, and I wanted a way to calm my thoughts. For several years, I had gone to learning specialists and therapists to improve my concentration and overall success in life. None of them could provide the change I sought.

My frustrations reached a pinnacle in my freshman year of college. Filled with partying, self-sabotage, and frustration, college moved me yet another step closer to failure. Little did I know, however, that the experience would change my life.

When I decided to take time off from school, I was fed up with life in America. I found many aspects of the culture morally, philosophically, and ethically repugnant. Of course, now I love America. But at the time, I wanted to go far, far away, to a place where no one knew me and I didn't know anyone. For no particular reason, I chose Dublin, Ireland.

During my stay in Ireland, I had scheduled regular phone conversations with a man named Dr. M. He was a psychiatrist by trade, my mentor in practice. He was the first person to tell me my brain functioned perfectly fine, and my "disabilities" originated from a skewed perception of my past. His non-diagnosis and dogged determination to convince me I didn't have, in his words, "AD Whatever," created a paradigm shift in awareness for me.

I was shattered, then, when my mother called me on Christmas Eve to tell me Dr. M had died of prostate cancer. I sobbed for hours. A feeling of helplessness consumed my entire being. I was alone in a foreign country, with no real friends to support me. I found myself hard-pressed to believe my life would ever improve.

After a few days, however, my perspective began to shift. Perhaps, I thought, I could reposition his passing as a blessing. He had given me the gift of self-examination, and now my job consisted of using that gift to turn my life around. After all, he always told me I would one day develop my own opinions, and they would, most likely, conflict with his.

I decided to pick myself up by the proverbial bootstraps, improve my life, and finally get over the mental blocks that were keeping me from success. The first step was, much to my chagrin, the self-help aisle of the bookstore. I was on a wild goose chase to end the infinitely frustrating cycle of procrastination and self-sabotage. I decided I had depended too much upon others for salvation, and self-help presented the only viable path to change. Yet every time I visited the dreaded *Section A* of my local bookstore, I felt overwhelmed with embarrassment.

Nonetheless, I persisted. And I'm grateful I did.

The first book I read was Wherever You Go, There You Are, by Jon Kabat-Zinn. Since I often felt my days were filled with mentally absent meandering, the notion of mindfulness appealed to me. As my interest in relaxation and stress relief grew, I began reading more books about Eastern philosophy.

I noticed how many of the books focusing on relaxation incorporated holistic concepts of mind, body, and spirit. Coming from a scientific, realist background, this was all a little "woo-woo" to me.

The way I grew up, if you had a headache, you took Tylenol. If you couldn't concentrate, you probably had Attention Deficit Disorder – or some other diagnosis in the DSM-IV. All this talk of spirituality, God, past lives, and synchronicity only confirmed my previous perceptions of tofu-eating, tree-hugging, New Age hippies who lacked any authentic grasp on reality.

The spiritual aspect of personal development seemed irrelevant. I just wanted to chill out, get focused, and finally turn my life around. Why I had to read all of this fluffy metaphysical literature to get there was beyond me.

Yet the more I explored metaphysics, the more I became fascinated with this mysterious and intriguing world. The authors challenged my previously insular perspective, pushing me to grow in new ways. And, over time, it worked. I started to see the world differently.

Maybe we weren't so separate after all. I could begin to see how a lot of the conflict in my life resulted from my own thought process. This was pretty cool stuff.

Today, I am grateful for having stumbled upon material that changed my life. But I think much of the literature in the marketplace correlating spirituality and success is misguided. There often is an attitude of "It's true for me, so it must be true for you. If this is how I and my colleagues succeed, then you must succeed in the same fashion."

I know plenty of materially successful people who are not spiritual. And I know plenty of spiritual people who are not materially successful.

I know a woman who is deeply connected to her spiritual guides, who reveal to her teachings about the abundant Universe, and yet she cannot pay the rent each month. I know a multi-millionaire who does not exercise, drinks fairly heavily, and has a tenuous relationship with his children.

Sam Walton went to church regularly, but credited his faith more to cultural identity and purposes of socialization than to deep religious feelings. He was a normal guy from Middle America who knew the value of the dollar and remained committed to delivering the lowest possible prices to his customers. He also left his family with the greatest financial legacy in America today.

A former friend of mine taught courses on spirituality, meditated on a daily basis, and owned a formidable collection of spiritual texts. He also stole several hundred thousand dollars from his employer and lost everything. Of course, according to him, he lives in a "neutral universe" that he has "created," and everything is just fine and dandy. He even looks forward to prison.

On a human level, his psychological reasoning is quite pathological. But on a metaphysical level, his argument holds true. In the court, however, I doubt his spiritual explanation would serve as sufficient evidence to pardon his crimes.

Don't get me wrong. I believe my spiritual and entrepreneurial evolutions are connected. But that's me. You don't need material to become spiritual, and you don't need spirituality to amass material. If you are spiritual, and you focus on an entrepreneurial goal, then perhaps your experience in meditation, focusing intention, and visualization will help you to achieve success more quickly. But spiritual practice, in my experience, is not a prerequisite to material success.

For instance, one day I was having a discussion with one of the hottest young traders in America. He and I were discussing our sentiments on making money. I asked him if he had ever read Think and Grow Rich by Napoleon Hill. He said he hadn't. I recommended it, and we went our separate ways.

I'm not sure if he ever read the book. But he was a hot trader before our conversation, and he's continued to stay red-hot after our conversation. He has one of the best track records of any small-cap trader in today's marketplace. And I think he credits his success more to his stochastic indicator system than divine intervention.

We both agreed there was nothing wrong with making money, and society would be better off if people viewed money in a more positive light. He may or may not be spiritual. He certainly was a nice fellow, and struck me as having positive motives for making money. And you know what? I would trust him with my investments more than a trader who claimed to have an energetic connection with the abundance of the universe but didn't have anything show for it.

When Curt Schilling, a star pitcher for the Boston Red Sox baseball club, pitched one of his all-time greatest performances, he credited his success to God. He said that he got out of the way and let God work his magic. He went beyond his ego and tapped into a potent spiritual resource. He found a spiritual program that works for him – different than mine, yours, and the next guy's.

If you choose to adopt spiritual doctrines that have a special meaning to you, then I believe you will experience a richness far beyond egotistical satisfaction. If exploring the relationship between quantum mechanics and the Law of Attraction helps you to focus your intention and achieve your goals, then stick with that program.

All of this analysis has led me to discover one truth: If I do something and it works, I do it again. And again. Until I find something that works better. And then I do that.

The most important aspect of my spiritual evolution is that I not get entrenched in one particular ideology. That I keep searching for new ways to see the world – through science, spirituality, psychology, economics, political science, and all other domains of human thought.

I know there are always new realizations I can have in any moment. I know there are aspects of history that can teach me about the present and help me plan for the future. I know there are still many areas in my life and business I can improve.

My divine discontent leads me on this path, this journey, this game. And along the way, I try not to take things too seriously.

2) In what ways do you incorporate your Spiritual Beliefs into day-to-day business interactions?

My 7 year-old cousin, an energetic second grader named Gabe, eagerly awaits his chance to launch the soccer ball over the roof.

With each failed attempt, he grows more frustrated. He kicks it too far. Then too low. Next, with the side of his foot. Now, with the edge of his toe. But never where he wants to kick it. His problem isn't a lack of talent. He's an adept athlete, adroit and nimble.

So his confusion as to why he can't kick the ball over the roof is understandable. I can see his frustration, and feel the need to come to his aid.

I tell Gabe that if he focuses on exactly what he wants – hitting the ball over the roof – he'll do it. It might take him a few times, but he'll get there eventually. I start demonstrating what a focused person looks and sounds like. He mimics me. I tell him to get ready, and give him a nice, slow pass. Lo and behold, the ball flies over the roof.

"It's like I just say something to my brain, and it does it!" he exclaims.

"That's right, Gabe. That's exactly right. If you just focus on what you want, you're gonna become a great soccer player," I reassure him.

"Okay," he confidently responds, "I'm gonna do it again." I kick him the ball – a slow, perfect feed. He lines up and…barely clears the ground. We try again. No luck.

"Gabe, I bet you were thinking, 'Man, I did it once, but there's no way I can do it again. I really don't want to hit this next one with my toes. I've gotta hit this ball over the roof, but I can't do it if I keep hitting it with my toes.' Right?"

Without hesitation, he answers, "Yeah. That's what I was thinking about."

"Okay. If you only focus on hitting it in the way that you know is going launch it over the roof, you'll do it," I tell him. "Now, remember. Focus. Ready?"

Gabe's level of focus visibly intensifies. His eyes are locked onto the soccer ball, a symbol of his athletic power and self-mastery. I kick him the ball again. As I expect, he clears the roof with ease.

Out of the next ten attempts, he either comes within inches or successfully clears the roof on at least six occasions. The only instances in which he misses entirely are when his father is watching or he is focusing on *not* messing up. Once the distractions leave the environment, he invariably clears the roof.

From this example, I could discuss the spiritual principles behind Gabe's success. I could talk about harnessing the power of the unified field of consciousness. I could delve into a deep discussion of sub-atomic particles, quantum mechanics, and the frequencies of thought manifestation. And often, in my writings and teachings, I do.

But really, does a 7 year-old need to study quantum mechanics and the creative process to understand that when he focuses on a goal, he will achieve it? No.

I, for one, find such discourses fascinating. I identify with the philosopher John Stuart Mill, who differentiated between "higher" and "lower" pleasures – with reading, thinking, and engaging in challenging dialogue grouped in the former category. I think the search for spiritual truth represents man's greatest quest. But it is not necessary for success.

In my day-to-day business and life, I enhance my experience of life with spirituality. I put various spiritual exercises to the test, and find the ones that work best for me. I know plenty of successful individuals who believe success is only a matter of vision and persistence. Some of them even think many spiritual teachings interfere with success. And they might be right.

For me, spirituality and success go hand in hand. I design my lifestyle to incorporate as many philosophies, strategies, and experiences as possible, for I find the concept of a universal truth endlessly fascinating and worth pursuing.

And often, the search is not at all pretty. Some "spiritual" people hope that all of their mishaps will just magically disappear. They want "good" to always win over "bad." Unfortunately, the universe doesn't quite work this way.

In fact, if our external lives were devoid of problems, challenges, and occasional misfortune, we would have no drive to improve ourselves and the world. In many ways, human spirituality emanates from a "divine discontent" with the conditions of our lives, businesses, and communities.

If something goes wrong with a business transaction, that's an opportunity for spiritual, personal, and financial growth. Spiritually, I can use the experience to find divinity in moments of conflict. Personally, I can improve my communication skills with customers and position the experience as an opportunity for learning. And financially, I can create a new system to avoid the problem in the future, resulting in increased sales and lowered costs.

One of authors who inspired me to think this way is Ken Wilber, founder of the Integral Institute. Mr. Wilber created the Integral model, which attempts to organize the many domains of the "Kosmos" as manifested in human thought and action throughout history. He identifies four quadrants – the "interior-individual," or psycho-spiritual matrix in each person, the "interior-collective," or shared values in communities, the "exterior-individual," or physiological makeup of each person, and "exterior-collective," or the exoskeleton of society, the environment, and the universe.

If one neglects any of these quadrants, the system will not function at peak performance. For instance, if your health, state of mind, and family are intact, but your business is underperforming, your entire matrix will be affected. Similarly, if you're materially successful, respected in your community, and relatively healthy, but you have much unresolved psycho-spiritual conflict, you undoubtedly, at some point, will experience pathologies in other areas of your life.

The Integral model reminds me that all opinions contain kernels of truth, and that my business, family, health, and environment are not mutually exclusive. By incorporating this – and other materials – into my business and marketing strategy, I can create the overall conditions for balanced success.

3) What is the single-most important spiritual practice that promotes peace and prosperity within your own life?

The most reliable and effective spiritual practice I use is a sound technology called Holosync. Created by Bill Harris of

Centerpointe Research Institute, Holosync uses "binaural audio" to create a harmonious environment in the brain. As many of my challenges were neuro-cognitive, I believe Holosync helped me to create a "better brain."

The added brain functioning has allowed me to access deeper meditative states on a daily basis. Our mind either prevents us from discovering or provides the foundation for spiritual realization. Holosync allowed me to access the latter, for which I am eternally grateful.

4) Imagine you are having a conversation with God (or the Universal creator or whatever name you prefer)... Share with us what is being said about the scope and future of Spirituality in the Entrepreneurial Business world.

Me: I am not as concerned with "spirituality," per se, as I am with business ethics and values. Our private sector rests at a values level conducive to profits, not profitable change. Some might consider profits and social change opposing values, yet I believe they are inextricably linked.

Universe: I agree, Sam. We cannot reach spiritual realization in the marketplace until our values transcend the current business climate. A spiritually realized economy does not eradicate competition – sports and business will always be predicated upon competition – but it approaches competition with a sense of higher purpose, an intentional motivation toward creating good in society.

Me: Exactly. So, if I may, Universe, based on this platform, let me continue our discussion with an interpretation of entrepreneurial history. And I promise not to bore you to tears. Just stay with me.

Universe: Surely. I'm all ears.

Me: As you know, the markets have existed through every historical period of man's evolution. Once man realized he and his fellow humans were an interconnected community, wherein the survival of each was dependent upon the other, he began developing systems for material survival. Yet his "spiritual" desire to live abundantly, with commodious surroundings and ample purchasing means, drove him to conquer, horde wealth, and exploit the weaknesses of others.

Do you agree?

Universe: I do – but I'd like to correct one point you made. This "spiritual" desire you speak of…it is more an egotistical desire disconnected from authentic spirituality than a truly spiritual goal.

Me: For the most part, you're right. But we also must remember that individuals in each epoch operated according to their corresponding values systems. For instance, though many spiritual teachers quote the Bhagavad-Gita as an enlightening text, Hindu leaders believed in the caste system. Were these teachers spiritually enlightened? Perhaps. But their values systems were not conducive to liberal democracy and economic freedom, both products of Western moral philosophy – and essential for modern entrepreneurship.

Universe: From your viewpoint, one might say spirit does not discriminate against values. And I agree. Tribesmen, evangelicals, New Agers, and Wiccans all have spiritual experiences. They all claim an intimate connection to a higher power. Indeed, some scientists have identified "God" centers and receptors in the brain.

Now, we've just made an important distinction – mainly, that values, economic systems, and political institutions must be factored into any discussion of spirituality and entrepreneurship in a modern context.

Some theorists say the markets alone will solve everything. But if you're a student of history, you know that, as the systems of exchange evolved, certain "entrepreneurial" individuals, or oligarchs, exploited markets to uphold oppressive social and political structures. The wealthy and powerful turned positive resources – markets, religious teachings, and social institutions – into oppressive vehicles to retain their stronghold on society's wealth. This was not "my" doing in a direct sense, but the doing of man as he learned to use free will.

Me: Our free will is both a blessing and a curse, isn't it? I find it interesting that, though our free will has perhaps evolved over the years, today we are learning to use freedom in ways more conducive to liberal democracy and economic equality than in the past.

As this is a discussion on entrepreneurship, let us consider human rights and ethics within the historical context of markets. On the one hand, you had the creators, and on the other, the workers. One group owned property; the other provided the means for property ownership. Through slavery, feudalism, and early capitalism, the oligarchs cleverly institutionalized ignorance in the form of suppressed language, thought, and association.

Universe: And, you'll notice, only recently have "entrepreneurship" and "spirituality" been universally available to those living in free societies. In many polities around the world, the freedoms you humans associate with entrepreneurship and spirituality only exist in a distant dream. Again, this not "my" doing, per se, but rather the evolution of your own free will.

Me: At some point, I think we will actualize our free will and consciously develop our values systems. This doesn't mean everything will be peachy keen in the future. If you look at human history, you'll find predictable peaks and troughs of optimism and pessimism, respectively, like tides of the ocean. But I'd like to think that each peak will reach continuously higher levels of personal and societal development.

Sure, technology has its costs and benefits. We've lost certain aspects of our social lives to email and television. The common criticism of our modern society as lacking in moral grounding contains much truth.

Yet I am an eternal optimist. I believe that each advancement in our evolution brings good things and bad things, but the good things get better. For instance, I can now publish a book online and make sales within a week. Small businesses are now competing on more equal playing ground with major corporations for advertising on the Internet. Access to information is at an all-time high with the advent of wireless technology. In many ways, these are previews of what a post-capitalist economy might look like.

These advancements can have both deleterious and advantageous effects on society. I can only hope we leverage technology not to replace spirituality, but to enhance our understanding of humankind's role in the development of history, consciousness, and spiritual evolution.

Universe: There is much truth to what you say. As entrepreneurs begin to develop their values, the marketplace will respond accordingly. You can use the marketplace as a tool, but be warned: You must create the conditions for global prosperity. The market won't "magically" do it through the hand of God.

Your economy functions according to the law of equilibrium. The marketplace constantly strives toward equilibrium in a divine struggle for supply and demand. We can look at equilibrium in two ways. First, there is the purely physical equilibrium in the goods market. But the other side of this analysis reveals a values-based equilibrium. The values of the consumers and firms determine both the practices and the products in the marketplace.

Today, as you know, our values-equilibrium indicates we have much work to do. And the entrepreneurs of this world have a critical role to play in the gradual development of this equilibrium. The trick is to make sure the values-equilibrium in each of our own lives can accommodate a global equilibrium greater than it is today. Only until the participants in the marketplace can develop their own values can the equilibrium itself evolve.

Me: You know, I always knew I liked you. You bring up many important points. Neither spirituality nor business alone can solve our society's problems. The task of creating a more enlightened marketplace requires discussions beyond the current mainstream thought, in both spiritual and business circles.

But we can do it. And we will.

* * * * * * * *

Sam Rosen *is a full-time college student at the University of Pennsylvania, entrepreneur, and creator of the Succeed Young Total Success System, available at* *http://www.totalsuccesssystem.com*.

"Remain open. There is something bigger than you know going on here." -- Iyanla VanZant

---

Bob Scheinfeld

1) New information reveals that 75%+ of the world's most successful people are profoundly spiritual in both belief and practice. Describe how your personal and business success has evolved through Spiritual Influences.

I must start out by defining the term "Spiritual." Spiritual is the word I use to define the specific set of invisible or "unseen forces" that shape what happens to us in our daily lives. To me, "Spiritual" is a very practical term, not a religious term, although it can be looked at that way and is by many people.

Working with this definition, I must say that <u>all</u> of my success in business and life can be attributed to my ability to tap into what I call "the Spiritual Power Center" to get the help I need to succeed, to come up with ideas, develop strategies and plans, execute those strategies and plans, find resources, network and hook up with other people, develop or find techniques, etc.

In fact, I've developed two bodies of work, ***"The 11th Element"*** and ***"The 7 Power Centers of Life"***, which center around the System I've developed for tapping into the Spiritual Power Center.

The core of that System was passed along to me by my grandfather who used it to build Manpower, Inc., from a simple idea into a Fortune 500 behemoth raking in billions of dollars a year and to live a lifestyle most people only dream about (Note: Manpower is the world's largest temporary help service and currently ranked #176 on the Fortune 500).

2) In what ways do you incorporate your Spiritual Beliefs into day-to-day business interactions?

To be successful in anything, you need help in the form of people, ideas, resources, techniques and strategies. There's no such thing as a "self-made" anything. That's a popular and ego-based myth. We all need lots of help to succeed, no matter how talented we may be.

No matter what results you want to produce in business, there are numerous people, ideas, resources, techniques and strategies to choose from that *could* theoretically help you do it. But which ones are the "right" ones or the "best" ones for you and your unique wants, needs and situation? How do you find them?

The amazing secret my grandfather introduced me to was a very different place to go to get the help we need to succeed and a system for asking for and receiving that help.

I always begin my business projects and work from the very humble position of admitting I don't know the best way to do anything and recognizing the need to ask for help to find the best ways.

I tap into the Spiritual Power Center to ask for help with all my business projects, tasks, problems, issues, goals, wants and needs. And I've learned the most effective ways to receive that help back once I've asked for it.

If I'm writing an advertisement, sales letter or a website, I ask for help to make it as effective as possible. If I'm confused about something, I ask for help to resolve the confusion. If I have an important business meeting or sales call, I ask for help to make sure that as much mutual benefit as possible is exchanged at that meeting. If I have an important decision to make, I ask for help to make the best possible decision. If I need to hire employees or contractors, I ask fro help to find the best ones.

I constantly tap into the Spiritual Power Center to get the help I need to succeed.

3) What is the single-most important spiritual practice that promotes peace and prosperity within your own life?

Applying ***The 11th Element*** System is the single most important spiritual practice that promotes peace and prosperity. Beyond that, I would say meditation and intuition, both of which I consider spiritual practices.

4) Imagine you are having a conversation with God (or the Universal creator or whatever name you prefer)... Share with

us what is being said about the scope and future of Spirituality in the Entrepreneurial Business world.

The world's most successful people acknowledge their reliance on Spiritual or "invisible forces" to produce results. They know that the "invisible world" is the source of whatever abundance they've been able to create.

However, many business people (even the ones who acknowledge the power of the Spiritual Power Center) aren't fully aware of all the power available within those forces, how to fully tap those forces, or the fact that those forces (and not what we do from the "physical" level) really shape all of the results we produce.

My conversation in this context would be about:

1. The excitement we both share with helping people awaken to these Truths.
2. How to best help people consciously and proactively tap into the Spiritual Power Center to produce extraordinary results, in less time, with less effort, and much more fun.

* * * * * * * *

Bob Scheinfeld
690 Berkmar Circle
Charlottesville, VA 22901
434-220-3440
support@11thelement.com

The following websites will be helpful if you want to learn how to tap into The 11th Element and the Spiritual Power Center:

http://www.11thelement.com
http://www.7powercentersoflife.com/

"For wealth is of the universe and it does not belong to us - we belong to it." -- Deepak Chopra

---

Steven E Schmitt

1) New information reveals that 75%+ of the world's most successful people are profoundly spiritual in both belief and practice. Describe how your personal and business success has evolved through Spiritual Influences.

My personal and business success has evolved through personally finding my own spirituality. I found it through meditation. If I had one gift to share with the world, I would share the gift of meditation.

Meditation is like plugging into an electrical circuit, you become energized.

You become more peaceful. It releases stress and is a doorway to our true self. I give all my business success, from finding my true self that guided me, to finding my purpose.

2) In what ways do you incorporate your Spiritual Beliefs into day-to-day business interactions?

My spiritual beliefs run my day to day life. I believe once we find our true self, we are then guided to fulfill our purpose in life. Our intuition is always guiding us to do the right things. Every day I find time to meditate, to become one with the God Force and that God force is in every single one of us on this planet.

3) What is the single-most important spiritual practice that promotes peace and prosperity within your own life?

Meditation. Once you learn to connect with your higher self, you will want to go there time after time. And once you learn that prosperity is not outside of you, that you are prosperous now, prosperity will show up in your life in wonderful ways.

4) Imagine you are having a conversation with God (or the Universal creator or whatever name you prefer)... Share with

us what is being said about the scope and future of Spirituality in the Entrepreneurial Business world.

Spend your time with like-minded friends and start to give more and more. Listen to your intuition about your business endeavours. Find your purpose and share it with the world.

Your Friend,
Steven E

* * * * * * * *

Steven E.
Creator of the # 1 Best selling Wake Up… Live the Life you Love series.
http://wakeuplive.com
562-884-0062

"Ordinary people believe only in the possible. Extraordinary people visualize not what is possible or probable, but rather what is impossible. And by visualizing the impossible, they begin to see it as possible." --Cherie Carter-Scott

---

Melanie Strick

1) New information reveals that 75%+ of the world's most successful people are profoundly spiritual in both belief and practice. Describe how your personal and business success has evolved through Spiritual Influences.

I would not be successful today without spiritual practice in my life. One of the key spiritual concepts I learned many years ago is **what I focus on expands**.

If I want more love, I focus on all the love in my life. If I experience any form of frustration, struggle, and poverty, then I must be focusing on those aspects of my life. The second spiritual concept is **–I am a mirror of that which I don't want to see**.

In other words, what I see in you that I don't like is a great mirror for my own blind spots. Third, with self-acceptance comes total liberation. These three principles have given me freedom from being a prisoner of victim-mentality and have positioned to live my life from a state of power and gratitude.

Ten years ago I was in a lot of emotional pain. I was climbing the corporate ladder and felt completely disconnected from the people I worked with and my jobs within the company. I felt like a square peg trying to fit into all these different holes, like a child's wooden workbench.

Nothing I tried fit me.

Other people were in charge of my life, where I spent my days and nights (because I traveled a lot back then) and all I wanted was the freedom to live my life MY WAY. I began a deep self-exploration of my relationship to God and myself. I was blessed with many great spiritual teachers, some in the form of boyfriends, some bosses, and some magnificent spiritual leaders. Through that exploration I began to realize how unique I am and how my gifts were so much more than what could be expressed in my current company.

Because I had experienced such a painful childhood, and had a "story to tell", I knew that I was supposed to be mentoring other people. I had been given a huge gift in my corporate life, I understood the way big businesses worked. I began to see that every step of my evolution was for a greater purpose, even if it was painful. I was able to see every challenge as an opportunity to grow, to learn and to become a stronger human being.

I felt so grateful for my new perspective on life, that I decided to use all these skills to help others achieve success. I've studied human potential and I have a greater understanding of why people do what they do. I can now live my life and run my business from a space of "detachment."

I don't take things so personally any more, and I know I am responsible for the outcome in my life. I have learned how to focus my conscious mind, and release the dark shadows that my unconscious mind clings to.

But most importantly, I've learned how to really be "Me" and accept myself deeply and profoundly. That in turn has allowed me to be a powerful mentor to others, to be a better friend than I ever believed I could be, and to be honest and integrity-based in my business.

2) In what ways do you incorporate your Spiritual Beliefs into day-to-day business interactions?

I use the power of conscious creation to direct my beliefs, which in turn correlates to successful outcomes in my business. I treat people with honor, truth and integrity. I build teams to accomplish my objectives based on their unique natural talents and I honor them for who they are. I believe that every "breakdown" is actually an opportunity for a "breakthrough" and therefore, we just handle problems. I have created, and helped other leaders create, value-based businesses. My business is 100% aligned with my values of Freedom, Truth and Community. When I am faced with a conflict or problem, I tend to look at it from the perspective of "who do I need to be to have a different experience here." It has allowed me to grow through some very difficult situations. And it has given me a way to retain a deep sense of confidence and power as a female leader.

3) What is the single-most important spiritual practice that promotes peace and prosperity within your own life?

The spiritual practice that promotes peace within me is truth telling -- being completely and totally honest with what I need to feel inner peace. However, the practice that has completely changed my prosperity consciousness is realigning my unconscious beliefs with my desired outcomes.

4) Imagine you are having a conversation with God (or the Universal creator or whatever name you prefer)... Share with us what is being said about the scope and future of Spirituality in the Entrepreneurial Business world.

This is a great question. I believe that God, that Universal Life Force, is constantly in communication with the collective consciousness of all humanity. Whether or not we are listening is another story. I know that Entrepreneurship is the force of the new human expression. The fact that so many people are leaving Corporate America to start their own business tells me that humanity is taking more responsibility for the results they crave.

From "*What is Enlightenment?*" magazine to mainstream yoga practice, to online networking centers like *Wisdom Business Network*, spirituality has influenced many of us who want to see the world change. I think most of my "conscious friends" are sickened by the state of business practices today. People who choose greed over right action are experiencing a short-sighted gain.

Many spiritual entrepreneurs are the seekers, those who are searching for answers in a world of chaos. There are a few of us who have decided to **be** the difference in the world. I think that is where the future lies, **being the difference we want to experience**. Being *that* leader, *that* business owner, *that* creator, *that* truth-teller. You see, as a seeker, you are addicted to the process of discovery but you don't always achieve success. It is more fun to be on the journey than to arrive.

What the world needs now are people who will walk the talk. We need people who will make the tough choices in the face of conflict, people who won't sacrifice their values, priorities or integrity for a short-term gain. We need entrepreneurs who are committed to doing the right thing whether it is popular or not. I'm not saying I can do this any better than the next person, but I do know that this is what the Universal Life Force is calling forth in those who are listening. As Mahatma Gandhi once said, "Be the change you want to see in the world."

* * * * * * * *

Melanie Benson Strick, The Entrepreneur's Success Coach
http://www.SuccessConnections.com
(877) 830-3139
14320 Ventura Blvd #222
Sherman Oaks, CA 91423

Learn the 5 Massive Mistakes that can put you Out of Business…and How to Avoid Them at www.successconnections.com.

"The idea that I could with my thinking and believing develop a fortune never entered my mind" ~Thomas Jay Hudson

---

Joe Sugarman

1) New information reveals that 75%+ of the world's most successful people are profoundly spiritual in both belief and practice. Describe how your personal and business success has evolved through Spiritual Influences.

In the early to late 70's I didn't know what spirituality was. It wasn't something I was very familiar with at all. I did notice though, that there were certain actions that you took that resulted in either a positive or negative force in your life.

In 1980 I wrote a book called "Success Forces". It listed six forces that I noticed, and when I followed them, success quickly followed. For example, one of them was honesty. When I was honest I had positive forces working in my favor and great things would happen around me.

When I was slightly dishonest, a little white lie or something like that, it created problems for me. I observed different approaches to achieving success and summarized them in the six forces.

I didn't realize that the book I had written was a book on Karma for businessmen. You're probably familiar with karma, cause and effect.

So that was my first experience with spirituality, without even realizing it I had developed a series of spiritual principals through my own school of hard knocks.

2) In what ways do you incorporate your spiritual beliefs, practices into your day-to-day lifestyle now?

Everything I do really is truly spiritually based. One thing I believe is that honesty is really important. I also believe humility is extremely important. In both of these are cosmic energies.

If you are humble and don't brag, you create positive forces at least good karma.

If you are just the opposite, you are just waiting to get chopped down.

Another principal is the principal of non-attachment. In other words I am not attached to any outcome. If it turns out great then that is wonderful. If it doesn't turn out very good, then I accept that. The reason I accept that, is I sincerely believe that everything that happens to you in your life is for your best interest.

Even in failure there is always a great deal to learn.

I also believe the more traumatic or more difficult life you have – the more powerful your energy is to manifest.

So that, even in very difficult times when things are really tough or you've gotten a major setback, you're setting the stage for building your energy to a point where you will be able to manifest things considerably easier.

The other thing is I've seen a lot of philosophy that people use in terms of spirituality.

One of the things I do, if I want something or really want to accomplish something, is visualize it in full detail. Picture what it will be like. Or what the payoff will feel like to get there. And then, here is the key, I forget about it. Release it. Let it go. Let the forces of nature take over.

When you want to accomplish something – or want something – visualize it, release it, then let it go.

That doesn't mean I don't pursue it, I work on it to make it materialize. I have found visualizing exactly what I want and then letting it go, comes with non-attachment. I am not attached to any outcome.

If I let that energy out there, it has a greater chance of manifesting if I thought about it, and did affirmations everyday.

I could blow bubbles into a soapy solution, and if I try to shape the bubble it would burst.

So, it is the same with the energy you are releasing to the universe.

You imagine something, picture it, visualize it, and let it go. And it, like that bubble - will form its perfect shape and carry onto the atmosphere and into reality.

Families and parents try to do the opposite of this to their kids. Sometimes they want them to be certain people. Try to shape them, bend them. Kids turn out to be psychos. If parents had left them alone and let them develop in just their own natural way, they would turn out to be great kids.

I personally don't meditate. I know it's recommended by a lot of people and it's in a lot of people's spiritual practice.

In the sense I do, in my own way. Maybe when I go to sleep or wake up in the morning. There may be a point in which I probably do something similar to mediation. But I don't consider myself someone who meditates.

Visualization and letting it go. The hardest part for most people

3) Is there anything I haven't asked; you would like to share with, with those who would be interested in this type of book?

One of the philosophies I have always had is <u>never give up</u>. There are so many times in life when you go through things, you fail, one after the other and you get discouraged.

The key is never to give up. The philosophy I always talk about is this: We are all given a bucket of oysters. When you try to open them up, if you know what it is like to open up oysters, can be quite difficult. You can scratch and cut yourself. Takes a little strength.

But in one of those oysters in the bucket you receive is a pearl.

That pearl is your big success.

The key is; some people will find it after the first couple of oysters. They're pretty lucky. Other people will have to open up most of the bucket.

Finally they come to the last oyster.

Point is: you don't give up. You just keep going. Those that give up will never find the pearl. It's there. And its there for the taking. You just have to understand, never give up.

* * * * * * * *

Joe Sugarman - Chairman, JS&A Group, Inc., BluBlocker Corp. and DelStar Publishing, Inc.

Joe Sugarman is one of America's top advertising and marketing entrepreneurs and the man who built several large businesses all through the creative power of his pen. He is more than an effective salesman, writer and marketer. He's an entertaining speaker, a great teacher and visionary marketer who openly shares his lessons learned from a lifetime of direct marketing.

The New York Times called him a "Mail Order Maverick," Bottom Line called him "One of the country's greatest copywriters," and Success Magazine called him, "One of the most successful direct marketing gurus of all time."

http://www.blublockers.com

"Strength does not come from physical capacity. It comes from an indomitable will." -- Mahatma Gandhi

---

Bob Switzer

How My Personal and Business Success Has Evolved Through Spiritual Influences

Success for me is having the qualities of life that are important to me present in my life each moment. Success starts with uncovering one's greater purpose, and then aligning their friends, activities, work etc. in harmony with this heart-felt desire. We can truly feel satisfaction from life by moving with our destiny, and this is something we feel.

Essentially, the more spiritually aligned my life has become; the more I have shifted from being a taker from life to a giver to life. I have been in this transition for over twenty years now and my mission in life at this point is focused on helping others grow spiritually in their business and personal lives so they can find a new balance for themselves and truly feel success in their lives as a result. Through my speaking, consulting and writing, my life is about helping others find what I have found, a new kind of success which can be described as spiritual freedom, an inner peace that is a blend of working, creating and serving all life at the same time.

I have learned that part of anyone's personal search for success today comes with a shift away from relying on the mind exclusively, to working with the gut, the heart and the mind (*the three minds* in the words of spiritual author Harold Klemp) in making our daily choices and moment to moment decisions. The focus of success then becomes one of feeling life as an experience as opposed to measuring it as assets, things or the number in our bank account.

Listening to my inner guidance using my three minds, the heart, gut and mind has become key to my success today in following my highest wisdom. The recent completion of my next book, **The Soul Perspective** was just such a journey of listening.

I had reached another stage in drafting the book, about a year after the initial structure was laid out and I was about at the three quarters point in the project when I got a very strong urge to stop. At first I did a very good job of ignoring this seemingly illogical message. I had just made a career change two years earlier from senior executive in the corporate world into becoming an author and speaker and I was totally dedicated to this new direction. Yet as I progressed each day, it became clear that I was pushing against the grain, I was trying to force the process. The heart was saying, STOP! But the mind was saying, if you stop, "What will you do?"

Nine months later, finally I got to the point where I could go on no further and I put the work away. I literally put all my notes and files in boxes and took them out to the garage. I knew that something was wrong with what I was doing, but what? I had been sensing the need for a move during this time frame and when I let go of writing this book and following a period of stillness, things started to break. I got the urge to put my house up for sale and to move to the ski resort community where my wife and I owned a ski condo. The city house sold quickly and I felt that my life was beginning to flow. Next we got the urge to sell the ski condo too! Within days of being on the market, it sold as well, another sign that we were in the flow of life and were headed in the right direction, but what direction? I felt like I was flying blind. We still had plans to live in the ski resort, but where? And what could I do there to earn a living?

My wife and I had dreams of building a log home so we ended up finding a great little five-acre homestead site, which we purchased. That ended up being another sign from spirit, as the property could not be found on the local multiple listing service and the site sign had fallen down. It was like the property was being held for us, just waiting for us to discover it. Things were really connecting but this whole process was taking a lot of listening and trusts in spirit on my part.

I still hadn't solved the earning-an-income part of the equation. I postulated the idea of being a log home dealer as the log home we wanted to build could serve as a model home as well. So I developed some contacts and did a lot of research in the log home industry. I now had a back-up plan of sorts but building a house was a nine to twelve month proposition in our new high-demand community.

As we approached the time when one would normally rent for the start date selected, I kept getting inner messages "not yet". (The only alternative was to pitch a tent on our newly acquired property, I had mused at the time.) Finally, I got the feeling that we could start looking three weeks before being homeless (but not landless). Instantly we ended up connecting with a beautifully renovated old Victorian home for rent in the center of town, a complete switch from the vision we had of chalet living near the mountain slopes where our new property was located. My wife and I immediately fell in love with the house and we signed the deal and moved in three weeks later. Interestingly, if we had forced the issue and tried to rent earlier, this house would not have been available any sooner because a previous rental agreement had fallen through at the last minute. This was another sign to me that my trust and patience and my ability to listen to my inner voice (my heart, mind and gut) was the course to follow.

Now I found myself settled in the new ski/mountain town, but what was I to do? Writing was out of the question, as this did not feel right. Within a week of getting settled, a friend who had moved here a year earlier knocked on my door. We had been brainstorming new ideas for four years on travel clubs, timeshare programs and private residence clubs. As he looked around and saw that I had just finished unpacking he told me about a real-estate opportunity near the mountain that would be perfect for our club project. I agreed immediately and wrote out a small deposit check. Another miracle: the deal to purchase this large tract of land included a one year closing, time for us to develop the concept and marketing, do the preliminary engineering and obtain project financing. Again, my life was connecting and I felt like I had opened up the right doors, but I still could not see where my life was headed.

In the following months I revelled in the project. It was what I loved to do, develop new concepts and bring them to market and this was a beauty, a Private Residence Club with a 9-hole golf course and clubhouse and, we decided to make the project an all log home community. My earlier personal research and contacts were paying off. I was excited and feeling that I had found my new calling.

Then it happened! Nine months later I woke up one day with the feeling that I had to leave the project. And, just like the last time, I did a good job of ignoring the feelings, but they continued to persist and get stronger. Finally, like the last transition, I could not ignore the message any longer and a few weeks later I decided to inform my two partners of my decision. It seemed crazy that I would leave an $80 million project just as it was getting off the ground, and all of the opportunity that it represented, but there was nothing I could do. I had to follow my inner guidance.

I spent two weeks winding down my responsibilities, turning them over to the others, all the while wondering what I would be doing next. I spent the next two weeks in an empty space, doing some soul searching and spending time each day in contemplation. It gradually came to me that I needed to finish the book, but I wanted to be sure. I had left that behind once before and I did not want to repeat a mistake, but as days went on it became clearer that this was my new direction, again!

As fate would have it (I believe there are no coincidences) I had been drawn into a workshop on how to write a book while attending a spiritual seminar four months earlier, and this workshop and Debbie, it's facilitator had started me thinking about my writing to the point where I was actively participating in the exercises in the session such as book formatting and marketing/positioning. I ended up speaking to Debbie about the title of this work-in-progress during the break, and it was at this workshop that she suggested to me the title, **The Soul Perspective**.

I then returned home and continued with my development project. It was then over the course of the following days and weeks I began to feel that I needed to move on from the project, until I could no longer ignore the inner message to leave. And so after telling my partners that I had to leave, it was Debbie that I called to see if she was available and interested in editing my book. She agreed and the writing journey began again.

It took only a few days working with Debbie for me to see why I had to put the book on the shelf for a year. I needed to see more clearly what was needed in the book to make it a good reader experience. As I complete the book, I am still following the inner direction, not sure what path this project will take and where it will lead me. It has been a real lesson in listening to Soul, to that inner guidance.

Following the heart takes a lot of guts and apparent risk, but for me, so far, so good. The main thing is that I love what I am doing! I feel like I am more spiritually aligned today than ever before, listening to my inner guidance.

Incorporating My Spiritual Beliefs Into Day-to-Day Business Interactions

In my past twenty years of spiritual study I have learned that this universe is organized under a number of "Spiritual Laws" much like our country is organized under civil laws. Discovering these universal spiritual laws and understanding them is an ongoing study, one of unfolding consciousness. As the Masters say, there is always one more step in our growth as Soul and in discovering more about the Creator and that Creator's love for us.

These spiritual laws that I have learned have become the foundation of my life and the way I live, interact with others whether personally or in doing business. These laws boil down to two primary laws in particular that have been crafted in their utmost simplicity by Richard Maybury as follows: (1) Do all you have agreed to do, and (2) Do not encroach on other persons or their property. (These 2 laws appear in his book, *Whatever Happened to Justice?*)

The other spiritual laws that are vital to me and serve, as guideposts in all that I do are best applied to living and doing business as spiritual qualities. These qualities include:

- Honesty with myself and others,
- Taking responsibility for all that comes into my life,
- Patience,
- Creating harmony in my environment,
- Being of service to others,
- Listening to my higher wisdom and the wisdom/ideas of others,
- Knowing that I have a greater mission than the traditional goals of life and living with heart as a result.

The final quality is love, which encompasses all of the above but also includes respect for others and their choices without judgment, having compassion and helping others succeed.

The Single Most Important Spiritual Practice That Promotes Peace and Prosperity in My Life.

The single most important spiritual practice for me began 20 years ago. At the time I was searching for something more, for truth. And I am still a truth seeker today but much further along my path of discovery and realization. I have come to understand that truth comes to us if we listen. That truth actually reveals itself from the inside. Truth is found by going inward, not through the things in our outer world like books, lectures, television and the thoughts of others.

Truth's source is Soul, our true identity. I have come to know that we each are actually Soul, a spiritual being having a human lifetime of experiences that are for our growth as Soul. So the awareness I have come to is that I need to strengthen my connection to Soul, because it is Soul that is connected to the source, or God.

I have also discovered that connecting to Soul requires dedication and practice. So I have developed a spiritual habit of giving myself time for active reflection each day. And this time forms a practice or exercise, a spiritual exercise if you will. This exercise is all about exercising my spiritual abilities just like I also exercise my muscles to keep them in top form. I believe that the common expression, "use it or lose it" is correct even when it comes to spiritual awareness.

So I dedicate twenty minutes to a half hour each day, first thing in the morning after breakfast to ask God what I should be doing that day. It gives me a higher focus to my day and keeps the connection with Soul strong. This connection is important to me because I now receive intuitive nudges all the time and it keeps me ever aware of this constant guidance. It helps me on an ongoing basis and allows me not to have to think my way through many issues, because the answers come intuitively from Soul. As stated earlier, I listen to my three minds, the heart, the mind and the gut. This is a big de-stressor for me, not having to think my way through life. I am able to rely on my higher guidance for most things.

I have a quiet place in the house with a comfortable chair that I use and I sit comfortably upright. I close my eyes and gently look at the screen of my imagination in the middle of my forehead. I work with a "mantra" sound that has ancient roots yet is known in other cultures in many countries around the world today. The sound is HU and it sounds like the man's name "Hugh". I say, whisper or sing this sound and it has the power to connect me more easily to Soul, and the creator or God. It actually raises my vibration so that I am in closer harmony to the source.

I also look for spiritual light and listen for spiritual sounds that can manifest when I am doing my "Spiritual Exercise" and if these appear, I follow them into a deeper contemplation. This has worked for me for over twenty years and provided me with spiritual insights beyond description and changed my life several times over.

You can gain a greater connection to Soul as well. Here is a suggestion to get you started. Find a time each day when you can be alone with your thoughts for 20 minutes without television, radio, or other forms of entertainment and the thoughts of others. You want to relax the mind in this time. This could be at lunch hour, when you get home from work, when you first get up in the morning, or just before bed at night. Consider this, your time, time you need to reflect on your life, your needs, your work, etc. Once you have found your time, you need to make a commitment to keep this date with yourself each day. This is your gift to yourself.

Now that you have your time set aside for just you, you are ready to access the power of Soul. While comfortably seated with your hands in your lap, gently place your attention on the screen of your imagination. Now if you would like to take this a step further, the sound of HU will help you tune in to Soul, your highest reality. This mantra and the vibration of this sound can give you a deep sense of relaxation and even provide profound results, insights into challenges and solutions. Try saying, whispering, quietly singing or even silently saying HU and it will help you tune in to Soul your highest reality. This sound is as ancient as the principles I describe in my book, *The Soul Perspective* and will take you far if you choose to use it.

The Scope and Future of Spirituality in the Entrepreneurial Business World

Over the course of my twenty years of spiritual study I have learned that, there have been many spiritual messengers that have come to teach us truth, among them Jesus, Buddha, Mohammed, Krishna, and Rumi. They all presented in their time and in their own way, the same basic universal message founded upon common spiritual principles. It is only the lesser human mind that has changed the message over the centuries. I believe that the guidelines or spiritual principles that these spiritual giants taught in their own times are gaining in importance in our world today and are becoming vital to personal and business success.

We are witnessing a huge spiritual shift that is gaining momentum in the Western world today and it is leading to many changes in what we value and how we interact. And, if you can see and understand the coming changes and "the new rules" these changes are ushering in, you will be able to move with them and change your approach to business and how you relate to others and this world. You will be able to create a new genuine wealth for yourself and your business and feel a sense of success far beyond your imagination. Of greatest importance, by your example you will be able to lead others with a new sense of vision as we move into this new era.

The changes most of us are aware of, to some extent or another, are the technological changes that are everywhere apparent. We are actually experiencing a quiet but rapid revolution as we shift to a new society that is totally supported by technology. In twenty years the world will be significantly changed as we adopt new enabling systems, and the children of the boomers, the "eco" generation, become the drivers of the new technology and its incorporation into our lives. These technological advances and changes will absolutely change the way that we do business and interact with one another in our personal lives.

The other dimension to this transition is human. We will have to change what we value (our values) in order to be able to use effectively, the gifts technology will bring us. The human ability to accept and integrate a shift of this magnitude will require a new adaptability and flexibility on our part, if we are to take full advantage of today's revolution in a way that will enrich our lives. In fact, we will have to change not only our view of ourselves and of our world, but also how we interact with each other in order to successfully integrate the new technologies into our lives.

The events of September 11th and following that date, have given us cause to pause and think about what is really important to us. What do we really value? What is at the core? Freedom, family, friends, and inner peace have all come to the surface for millions. How we interact with each other and how we treat each other is really at the core of our values and our existence. As we shift into the new age how we respond to life and its challenges will be vital to our well being, business success, and our very survival.

The shift in our core values that is occurring in our society is in part a reflection of wanting to be more than simply survivors or money-makers in our lifetime. Many in our society, have started to look inwardly for answers to life's deepest questions and are discovering that there is a greater meaning to life, if they open themselves to that possibility. In essence, they are becoming aware of their own spiritual nature and this shift is moving our whole society toward being spiritual-values driven. Witness the mass advertising today that pictures men in yoga classes, uses the humor of past lives and reincarnation and includes themes of revelations and dreams to catch our attention. In addition, television shows like *Crossing Over* and Oprah are bringing spirituality into the mainstream as well as a growing number of spiritual books and lectures.

And so the seed urge to discover our spiritual nature, buried deep within our hearts is now emerging. In the optimum scenario, the technological changes will give us the time, ability and freedom to pursue this quest for personal growth. More importantly, the new technologies are actually causing a values shift that is changing the paradigm.

This means the rules are changing! My belief is that we cannot expect to solve our personal, business or global challenges with the same thinking and responses that got us to our present circumstances. We need to get out of the old "industrial age" box and take a different view of life. We need to be creative, seek a higher view and work with new principles, new tools. The convergence of technology and spirituality is symbiotic in that each of these movements requires the other in order to lead us into the new society that I believe we have the opportunity to create in the coming years. The new technological revolution is being enabled by our shift in values and, conversely, as we adopt the new technology, we are being given the opportunity to shift our values and grow as a society and as individuals. To do this we need to learn the discipline of using the new technologies such as cell phones and email as aids to giving us greater freedom to work from this higher perspective and conversely not to let them run our lives.

The values that are becoming important to personal and business success today include trust, honesty, respect, freedom, caring, forgiveness, listening, harmony, giving and many more. All of these I refer to as Spiritual Values. The wellspring of these values is the common spiritual principles that have been brought to us by many great spiritual teachers and masters and it is this universal message that we are now discovering in our own time and in our own individual ways. These ancient and timeless principles are now manifesting in the business world and are becoming essential practices for success in our changing world. (These spiritual principles and how they are manifesting today as keys to success is this the message of **The Soul Perspective**, my next book.)

And so the success of each of us today and going forward is wrapped up in our ability to understand and apply key spiritual principles in all that we do in business and in our personal lives and to employ the new technologies to our benefit to give us greater freedom.

* * * * * * * *

Bob Switzer is and Speaker, Business Consultant and Author of *Business & Social TrendZ, Profiting With Spiritual Economics.*

His next book, *The Soul Perspective* will be released in 2005. He would love to hear your stories and realizations relating to your discovery of working and living with higher values (Spiritual Principles) and how this has benefited you or your business or brought you new levels of success. Contact him at GRobertSwitzer@Rogers.com and he will email or call you back.

"Don't make excuses -- make good." -- Elbert Hubbard

Monique Thomas

1) New information reveals that 75%+ of the world's most successful people are profoundly spiritual in both belief and practice. Describe how your personal and business success has evolved through Spiritual Influences.

From "mouse" to "I am woman, hear me roar". Literally. Blending spirituality into my business and personal life saved my life. I don't even want to imagine where I would be if I hadn't.

It all began by understanding myself and changing the things that limited me in life by making wiser choices. This applies to any aspect of life, business or personal.

We are all spiritual beings made up of energy or elements that become or transform us from the choices we make.

Instead of choosing failure, I chose success. I determined that I would succeed no matter what. It required a deep commitment on my part and getting out of my comfort zone. It also required me to define it for myself, as it is a very personal and individual thing for all of us.

Success is an element within us all, inborn, inherent. It doesn't happen overnight but the potential is there. It's not something you reach, for there is always more. You grow into it, step by step.

I needed to change my perspective. Where I saw only problems before, I began to see opportunities, answers, and solutions and apply them to my personal and business life. My thoughts and emotions gradually changed to provide me with a more positive, productive and successful mindset. My abilities have definitely expanded into areas I never would have even considered ten years ago.

Spirituality has given my life purpose, passion and direction. When you know where you're going, focus is easy. It has allowed me to have more open, honest, loving relationships, business or personal.

And it has definitely improved the quality and richness of my life versus accepting the mediocrity of the life I lived previously.

We truly do create our own reality and success is something I chose persistently and consistently. Sometimes I fell off the wagon but I always got back up.

Never give up.

2) In what ways do you incorporate your Spiritual Beliefs into day-to-day business interactions?

As I am made up of elements of energy, what I do is very simple. I program it to be what I choose.

Before doing anything, I decide what element I need to bring into the project or actions I am taking. It might be the element of success, creativity, abundance, positivity, confidence, etc… Then, I let myself see, feel and experience that element for a time, really bring the emotion of it to the surface, to my consciousness. Next, as I go about completing the project or task, this essence goes into the actions that I am taking. In other words, I am bringing my heart, soul and spirit into everything I do.

The amount of work that I accomplish and the speed with which I complete it still amazes me.

3) What is the single-most important spiritual practice that promotes peace and prosperity within your own life?

I find that simply remaining focused on what I truly am, throughout my day, the elements, the essence of what I am, the positives, is the simplest and most important practice for me. It reminds me of what I am and keeps me from getting tangled up in the negatives. It literally carries me through my day.

4) Imagine you are having a conversation with God (or the Universal creator or whatever name you prefer). Share with us what is being said about the scope and future of Spirituality in the Entrepreneurial Business world.

There is definitely no limit to what can be achieved when you 'marry' the spiritual to the entrepreneurial business world. You can even see it emerging as we speak. The level of creativity that you can achieve is still in its infancy. If I told you the scope of it, you wouldn't even believe me for it is a future that hasn't been imagined yet by the human mind. Oh, you have flirted with that dream, but not yet realized that you can actually make it real.

Without spirituality, it is a future that will never be. Imagine a marketplace that is open and honest, more ethical in its practices. A marketplace where anything less than the best just simply will not do and where mediocrity is a thing of the past. Quality versus quantity.

Entrepreneurs connect people to people, for without them there is no business. I would ask that each one of you look into your hearts and take more care with what you produce. Bring spirituality into all your dealings, projects and products and you will experience more success than you ever dreamed possible. And, as is already apparent, more and more people will achieve this success.

This will have and already has begun to have a global effect on your world as the line between the haves and have-nots begins to disappear.

It requires change, more importantly it requires people to change. As you do, so too will the business world and all other aspects of your world.

* * * * * * * *

Monique Thomas
9813 93 Ave
Grande Prairie, AB
Canada
780-532-1854

Monique Thomas is the owner of http://www.thelovequotecollection.com, executive director of http://www.livinginpowerandwisdom.com and editor of 'The Spiritual Solution Newsletter'.

"You are the universe. It is not something outside you. You are that force which is in everything." - Wayne Dyer

---

Carol Tuttle

1) New information reveals that 75%+ of the world's most successful people are profoundly spiritual in both belief and practice. Describe how your personal and business success has evolved through Spiritual Influences.

I know without a shadow of a doubt that my success is because of my spiritual practices. I believe faith is the power that creates. My faith in God, the possibilities, and myself is what has made the difference.

I believe that faith without works is dead, so I lead with the faith and follow-up with the works.

As I am led by the spirit, I am inspired as to what I am to do. Faith is my primary principle in my spiritual business model. Faith, free of doubt in moving ahead to create a multi-million dollar enterprise with the primary benefit of helping my customers create miracles in their lives. I am definitely on my way.

2) In what ways do you incorporate your Spiritual Beliefs into day-to-day business interactions?

I pray on a daily basis for guidance in managing and growing my business. I believe God wants my business to prosper and is desirous in assisting me in that outcome. I ask specifically in my prayers that my business will be blessed to be fruitful and successful.

I practice creation and manifestation techniques in helping create my success. I do a process called energy circles where I stand in front of an imaginary circle and throw powerful affirmation statements in to the circle, step in the middle and dress myself in the energy.

I also believe that angels and guides are assisting me and I call upon their aid daily. I ask them to help me reach the people I am meant to help or who are looking for help all over the world. Since much of my business is internet based I ask my angels to bring people to my websites that will benefit from the resources available there.

I work in the field of Energy Therapy where much of my work is helping people clear their negative energy, so of course I am using techniques to clear my own negative energy on a daily basis.

3) What is the single-most important spiritual practice that promotes peace and prosperity within your own life?

Prayer - talking with God on a daily basis and receiving inspiration and personal revelation to make the choices that will create the highest good.

4) Imagine you are having a conversation with God (or the Universal creator or whatever name you prefer)... Share with us what is being said about the scope and future of Spirituality in the Entrepreneurial Business world.

Dear Heavenly Father,

Thank you for assisting me in being a role model for others to come into their light and truth. I am grateful that spirituality is reaching all areas of life on our planet. Thank you God for assisting my business in growing in reaching millions of people who are looking to relieve the pain and suffering.

I believe that we are coming to a remembrance of our God self, our characteristics that are God-given. I believe God wants us to be successful and has engaged all the powers of the Universe to aide us in this outcome. Business is just one experience in our lives. I believe that we are meant to resource and benefit from our spirituality in all aspects of our lives, it is natural for me to practice my spirituality in my business model.

I believe the businesses that incorporate a spiritual practice and stay in integrity with the vision God has for us, will be the most successful.

5) What hasn't been asked that should have been addressed or answered?

It is a common misconception that if you operate from a spiritual model, money cannot be a part of it. The illusion that if you do well financially, in business, the business does not have a spiritual foundation. This is a result of people still believing money is not spiritual. I believe money is one of the most spiritual commodities we have on the planet. It can do tremendous good and create incredible change for the better. I believe God would much rather have us wealthy and humble, willing to do his will, than poor and humble, without much resource to do his will.

It is important to keep in perspective why we have created our businesses. Too often the motive comes down to money. I keep my priority of helping people change their lives as my key value and feel completely in integrity that I profit financially for this exchange.

I invite you to experience the Money Clearing Session on my interactive website, "The Carol Tuttle Energy Healing Learning Center, "to assist you in clearing up your money energy.

* * * * * * * *

Carol Tuttle is an energy psychologist, best-selling author, and very successful speaker. She has appeared on hundreds of radio shows and many television appearances. She and her husband, Jon, reside in Salt Lake City, UT and utilize these energy-clearing techniques in their everyday lives with their family of 5 children.

Carol's book, "Remembering Wholeness" and her other products are available on her website http://www.caroltuttle.com. In addition she has launched the Carol Tuttle Energy Healing Learning Center, an interactive website utilizing these techniques for clearing literally hundreds of issues. You can visit that site at http://www.caroltuttlelearningcenter.com

"Nothing Paramount Has Ever Been Achieved Except By Those Who Dared Believe That Something Inside Of Them Was Superior To Circumstance." – Bruce Barton

---

Joe Vitale

1) New information reveals that 75%+ of the world's most successful people are profoundly spiritual in both belief and practice. Describe how your personal and business success has evolved through Spiritual Influences.

I owe all of my success to my listening to, and following, my spiritual impulses. That may come as a shock to a lot of people who may say, "oh, you got an idea, you wrote something and got lucky. Or, you did a lot of promotion and that's why it sold. There are all kinds of excuses and logical explanations that people can offer.

From my window seat, what I do is tune in to my intuition, which for me is my direct phone line to spirit.

What I am suggesting is that I listen to a deeper whisper that seems to come through my feelings which is my connection to all that is. You know, "this is bigger than Joe's ego." This is Joe connected to the universe. I listen to it and when it says something, I pay attention.

Here is a concrete example, I remember a Christmas, twelve years ago, and I was reading the Robert Collier letter book, which was a dramatic book that deeply influenced, transformed, and altered my life as a writer. In it there was a mention of someone named Bruce Barton. You know other people have read that book, but nobody else had the signals that told them to pay close attention.

Why?

It was no conscious reason that said, "Maybe you should take a close look at this, go and explore Bruce Barton." I began a quest that took a couple years and ended up with me writing a book called "The 7 Lost Secrets of Success".

One person so loved that book they bought 19,500 copies of it and that book is still included in my Nightingale-Conant package, "The Power of Outrageous Marketing." Clients can buy the package and they get that book as well.

My point is, this is why its so relative, I did not think consciously, " I should study this Bruce Barton and write a book that's going to be a best seller, stay in print for 10 years and be loved by many". That was not in my mind.

What was in my heart was, "I'm really curious about this man and I'm going to explore this and see where it leads." This was a very different strategy. Instead of coming from a logical strategy that says, "Hey you can write a book and make money from it", it was more of a spiritual impulse that said, "explore this man and we'll tell you why we want you to explore this later".

I owe it all to paying attention to spirit every day.

2) In what ways do you incorporate your Spiritual Beliefs into day-to-day business interactions?

I do it on every level and in every interaction. Now don't mistake or think that Joe is a walking perfectionist, I'm not. I'll often forget to meditate or I'll often ignore my intuition and many times I'll end up regretting it. I learned over time and through trial and error, I'm far better off when I pay attention to those impulses.

So, I do it on every level.

When I check my email, and I get hundreds of them in a day, I look for an intuitive impulse or an intuitive "yes". Here is an example. I hear from people all the time who have book projects, or software projects or joint venture requests and they want me to be a part of it. I always look at this from numerous levels. From a logical sense, I ask "does this make sense" and from a marketing level "is there a market for it?"

But, I predominantly look at it from a intuitive/spiritual level and ask, "is my inside connection to all that is saying –yes, this is a match for me in my life."

Most of the time, these projects that come through are not a match for me in my life and I end up saying "No, I cannot do this project. I wish you well. Go out there and burn up the world. Go make some sales. Just not with me."

Here is a real live example.

Last Saturday morning I got an email from a woman in Canada who wrote me this nice email. She's a big fan and has read all of my stuff. I didn't know who she was. She was working on a book on blogs and this thing called RSS. She wanted to know if I wanted to be a co-author and was wondering if I would at least look at it and give an endorsement. Something in my gut said yes, look at this. So I wrote back to her saying yes, please send it over and I'll have a look . She sent it over.

At this point it was a very rough draft, more like an outline than a finished book. But, my gut was saying this is really good, add to this and become a co-author. Flesh this book out. Well, I completely changed my plans for that Saturday. I sat down for hours and started re-writing her book. At the end of the day, she was ecstatic. Rather than a one-line endorsement she was thinking of, now I was her co-author. I worked with her on that book, off and on, for that entire week.

Now it's Friday, almost one week later and we're going to be releasing this book as a co-authored, joint ventured project, probably next week. From her standpoint, she thinks she won the lottery. From my standpoint, all I am doing is following my gut, my intuition, my spiritual call – it said, "hey, work with this woman, this is a great project, opportunity and she is a great lady." It is very important to work with good people. So, all those yeses were coming from spirit, my gut, and my intuitive signal. When you asked me to do this interview, I also asked the same questions, "is this good for me to do? Is there a market? Is it good for me to work with Troy?"

If all the answers are yes, then here we are.

Most people think you can't judge a person, a personality and their values by email. I totally disagree. I think emails are very revealing by what they say, what they don't say and most importantly by a feeling, spiritual level.

That message is there if you quiet down and pay attention to it.

3) What is the single-most important spiritual practice that promotes peace and prosperity within your own life?

Great question. I don't get to talk about this very much. I have completely re-written my spiritual marketing book. It's going to be out by John Wiley publishers by next March with a new title, it's twice as big, and I get to talk about this aspect a little more in the book. Here is the one thing that I do that I think is very different than most people and I think it is something that anyone can do.

I take what I call inspired action. Now most people know how to take action. Most people don't take action, which is a problem in and of itself. Inspired action is taking action that is propelled from an impulse within yourself, not from your logical mind, but from your intuitive mind.

For example, if someone wanted to start a new business selling socks on the internet, or magic tricks, or love potions on the internet, whatever it happens to be. Typically, from a logical standpoint they will look at the research material on how to start your own business. Probably they will write a marketing plan. Create some type of advertisement. Probably look at some yellow page ads. They come from a logical mindset that says this is how you start a business. And there's nothing wrong with that.

However, what I do is look within myself and say, "alright, this is what I want to do. I want to start this business or create this product. What is the best approach for me to do this successfully?" I tune in, and wait for an answer from a deeper level. That answer may be an impulse that says – call Troy. Or, it may be an impulse to write an email to Joe Sugarman. It may be to write a business plan. Or it may be go to the retired business people group SCORE and get some free advice.

The point is – it will be unique to you. It may, or may not, include those logical things like writing the ad or marketing plan. It may even be completely different. But what I am suggesting is that when you get this impulse from within, that's the inspiration part, then take action. So if there is any one thing I am doing, I am paying attention to the opportunities and impulses, the intuition that's coming up within me and then I jump on them!

One thing I've learned from Dan Kennedy is that money likes speed.

So when I get an idea for something or example the email I received last Saturday morning from a woman who wants a testimonial. I ended up being a co-author and am writing the book that day. Money likes speed.

I'm in a mastermind group and I met with them yesterday and was telling them "last Thursday, I didn't even know what RSS meant. This Thursday I am in a book as a co-author that explains it and how to use it in your business.

Money likes speed.

But it also came from me taking what I call inspired action. I got an inspiration to act, and then I took the action.

That's one of my big secrets!

Follow that intuition and pay attention to the signals that are coming to you. When it says take action – take action. You don't question it, you don't doubt it, you don't drag your feet.

You take action.

4) Imagine you are having a conversation with God (or the Universal creator or whatever name you prefer)... Share with us what is being said about the scope and future of Spirituality in the Entrepreneurial Business world.

Beautiful question. I will say what surfaces here without editing it.

This would be an encouragement. Joe, the business world is struggling. They are being overwhelmed and confused by the amount of information that is coming out. Internet, news and books – you name it. Most of it is conflicting as well.

So they stay in a state of perplexity – not knowing what to say, do, road to take.

So, all of these people in business really want to do good for themselves, for their customers, for their business in general. They want to make a profit but they also want to make a difference and are open to new ways of doing it. The universe would tell me "Joe, don't be afraid to walk into any one of these business and say, "there is another way to accomplish this". Then speak to them about the five steps to spiritual marketing, or about inspired action, or about teaching them to meditate.

To learn how to get quiet so they can listen to that inner voice. The more they do that, the more they'll see a softening of the rough edges in their business, the more they'll see a happiness in their business among themselves and their fellow workers, employees and customers. And the more they will see a natural profit, not fighting tooth and nail for but a profit that flows to them because they are in the flow.

Wonderful question that really makes you think, something for regular reflection on.

5) What hasn't been asked that should have been addressed or answered?

I would say the average person doesn't realize the power they have.

What I mean by that is that most of us have our physical power and whatever we feel our mental power is. But that's within the limits of our egos. If we would join forces with spirit then we've not doubled our power, we have multiplied it in some factor that I don't even know how to calculate.

What I am suggesting is that we set more intentions for what we want to achieve in life. Pay attention to what we want on the inside. We have what our ego desires but balance that with whatever is coming up within you. You may want to make a difference in the world and not just in your pocket book.

Though, there's nothing wrong with that. Wealth is good. I would say that instead of struggling to achieve it, set an intention that you're going to joint venture with the universe.

That your ally is spirit.

That your partner is this energy that is within all of us, that connects all of us. So, you're your are not the Lone Ranger going out there to capture the bad guy. You're actually part of this giant team and you are going out there to make this positive difference in everyone's life.

So I would say, set more intentions and realize you are not doing it alone. Pay attention to the inspired action that keeps coming up. And of course – take action when you notice it.

And realize that you are joint-venturing with universe.

* * * * * * * *

Dr. Joe Vitale is the world's first Hypnotic Marketer. He is President of Hypnotic Marketing, Inc., and author of way too many books to list here, including the #1 best-selling book "Spiritual Marketing," the best-selling e-book "Hypnotic Writing," and the best-selling Nightingale-Conant audioprogram, "The Power of Outrageous Marketing." His latest books are the best-selling "The Greatest Money-Making Secret in History" and "Adventures Within." His main website is http://www.mrfire.com

"You will become as small as your controlling desire; or as great as your dominant aspiration" – James Allan

---

Sharon Warren

1) New information reveals that 75% of the world's most successful people are profoundly spiritual in both belief and practice. Describe how your personal and business success has evolved through spiritual influences.

On some level, I was born instinctively knowing things were often not as they appeared to be. I always had a curious and adventuresome nature and my middle name could have been "why," as I asked endless questions. I ran away from school the first day, but the principal called and my mom discovered where I was and sent me back. Apparently, I intuitively knew what was in store for me in a traditional system. In retrospect, I also feel empathy for the ministers in churches I attended as a young girl because I challenged the status quo there too. For me, religion was what "authority" figures believed and imposed from outside influences, while my personal spiritual guidance and beliefs evolved from within.

My personal credo would become - trust my gut and follow my heart. As I matured, I learned that Joseph Campbell had wisely called it, "Follow your bliss."

"It is only with the heart that one sees rightly;
what is essential is invisible to the eye."
Antoine De Saint-Exupery

I was an insatiable reader, inveterate seeker and traveled worldwide as an adult. Being in other cultures added immensely to first hand experiences of spiritual influences and observing business practices. Little did I dream that a trip to Bali in 1996 would be the ultimate catalyst to write my book, "Magnetizing Your Heart's Desire". Contrast (challenges) definitely was initially afoot for our group's journey. It became an exquisite "set up" for what would unfold into new personal understandings and insights about life's "opportunities" (often known as "problems" depending on one's perspective). We can see things as an "upset," or as a mirror, which reflects a "**set up**" for our personal growth and evolution. The choice is always ours.

I've learned that contrast presents different perspectives through a mirror of "opposites." New decisions and choices are then born with greater clarity. We become more skilled by knowing what feels good and focusing on what we want in our heart of hearts whether it is with family, business, relationships, love, home or money. How we **feel** is always our point of attraction whether it be in our personal, business or spiritual life.

We lived in Indiana for twenty-three years. As a former Hoosier, I was very familiar with the Indy 500 car races and the black and white flag symbolism. It means "contrast" or slow down. In other words, always be aware of what you are **feeling**. Most of us know in basic physics that like attracts like. Simply stated, good feels good and bad feels bad. The Universe is always giving us clues and feedback which energy we are vibrating and emitting in our personal or business lives. That is our spiritual influence and guidance from within that succinctly reveals how we are flowing energy.

It is important to choose what empowers us and feels good because that is our signal for the Law of Attraction in Action. The power and speed of magnetizing our heart's desires is always through our pure, positive, passionate, penetrating emotions. Our emotions are literally our energy-in-motion of what we are now creating. As we think, we vibrate. As we vibrate, we attract. Our thoughts and emotions feed, vibrate, pulsate and radiate in every area of our life—negatively or positively in business and our personal life. They are indelibly intertwined. That is my spiritual guidance, as I always know when I am vibrating JOY I am connected to Source and my inner being.

I believe my greatest contribution both personally and professionally is being spiritually connected. As the expression goes "walking our talk." My greatest value to others and myself is when I am joyful and plugged into Source. I am then living, oozing and vibrating Well Being. I also believe personal and professional success means lightening up, as a sense of humor is an essential ingredient to our joy vibration.

2) In what ways do you incorporate your Spiritual Beliefs into day-to-day business interactions?

Creation Is About Attraction

I write daily in a personal gratitude journal because I believe having an attitude of gratitude is essential to our Well Being. What we think about expands. Appreciation is the fastest tool for personal growth and expands us into becoming more of what we are personally, professionally and spiritually. I also have various tools I have integrated which serve me well. One of them is simply sitting comfortably in the silence and quieting my thoughts so I become aware of my inner being. Walking meditatively in nature also enhances my connection to Source. Journaling and writing ***Letters To God*** is another avenue that enriches my life, as well as the ***I CREATE MY DAY*** process, which I will expand upon later in the segment for question three. I also find the ***BECAUSE*** process very effective and compelling for molding my day and life.

In my book, ***Magnetizing Your Heart's Desire***, the four steps of Deliberate Creation are outlined, from a personal interaction with Abraham Satarcia in 1998, which are amazingly simple and life changing. They are precisely and exquisitely how I incorporate my day-to-day business interactions with my spiritual beliefs:

Step One of Deliberate Creation

The first step of deliberate creation is to know what you do NOT want. Contrast is very important to our physical life. Without up, there would not be down. Without dark, there would not be light. Contrast is what creates the physical world. It is only through contrast that we can make decisions and it is only through decisions that you can create.

Step one in creation is to become aware of what you do **NOT** want. By knowing what you don't want will burst forth the clarity of what you do desire. Never do you want wellness more than when you feel ill. Never do you want abundance more than when you feel poverty or lack. Deliberate creation in step one is in knowing what you do not want. You do not want to stay focused there because prolonged attention to what you do not want can also attract that which you do not want into your experience. Step one is only to help you become clearer and so you begin to think in the direction of what is desired.

Step Two of Deliberate Creation

In step two for deliberate creation, you begin to think about what you do desire and you feed that energy. You feed that energy into what you deliberately desire to create. As you think about it, you reach into this vast repertoire of thoughts and senses that you have created through your lifetime. Every experience you have ever had through your senses—sight, sound, taste, touch, smell—any emotion you have ever experienced exists forever. You have a vast sensorium of emotions so in the deliberate creating process you begin to get clearer and clearer about what you desire. You bring forth bits and pieces of senses to create an emotion, which creates a feeling and a response. And as this energy becomes familiar to you, the sensation and emotions becomes stronger and stronger.

Step Three of Deliberate Creation

In step three of deliberate creation, you create a vibrational match to what you desire through emotion. This is very important to know and remember: **THE POWER AND THE SPEED OF ATTRACTION IS THROUGH YOUR EMOTIONS**. And you know, whenever you have been angry or frustrated with something that you can literally shake. When you are excited, or you are anticipating something that is a thrill to you, you may also physically shake from excitement and the sheer JOY of it. That is the power of vibration and the power of emotion. Emotion is always the key to the power and the speed of what it is you desire and your connection to your Inner Being and Source.

When you feeeeel the emotion of deliberate creation, you know you have clicked in, you feel the YES! YES! This is what I want! YES! This is what I desire, YES! And then you hold that vibration for 17 seconds, plus 17 seconds, plus 17 seconds, plus 17 seconds and you have created your launch! This older, wiser part of you is a wondrous guidance system from Source. It is a miraculous guidance system because this guidance speaks to you at every moment through your emotions. Because our brain mechanism moves very, very quickly, it is almost impossible to think two thoughts at one time. It is not possible to think a thought and realize, "I am thinking a negative thought." Your Inner Being communicates with you through emotion in every moment so you always know what feels good.

You can feed and energize good feeling thoughts until they become a tidal wave. As you know, you were born with an Inner Being, which is an older wiser part of you. There are many names for it. Some call it Soul or your Higher Self or Source. Ask your Inner Being or Source to assist and co-create with you. Always move toward that which feels good to you. In other words, follow your heart. When you look for reasons to feel good, you will find them. You are then resonating with your greatest power from a broader perspective.

Step Four of Deliberate Creation

Step four of deliberate creation is not your work. The how, the when, and the where are the work of the Universe, the work of this powerful Force. What you do is tell the Universe what you want. How do you know when you are in the flow? EVIDENCE ABOUNDS! Step four of deliberate creation is looking for evidence where your heart's desires have been fulfilled. Relax into the goodness of joyous well-being and gratitude.

Energy Wave Patterns Which One Are You Riding?

There are Only Two Feelings of Emotions

One Energy Feels Good and One Feels Bad

When you are feeling bad, it is your inner guidance tapping you on the shoulder telling you that you are standing in step one of deliberate creation. You are feeding energy into the wave pattern that you do NOT want to create. When you find yourself in step one, do not spend much time there. Do not be beat up on yourself when you are back in step one, which is only to bring clarity when you have challenges. Simply acknowledge any misadventures and say: Thank you Guidance System. Bless you!

You will know by your inner guidance system when you're slipping into step one of deliberate creation. You know exactly what to do about that. It takes you 17 seconds. It may take you a few minutes to say, "Oops, what is it again that is really my heart's desire? I want this to be easy and effortless." If you are thinking about when, where and how—or, like how are we going to fix this problem, you're back in step one. That's not your work, because after you have matched the vibration through your Inner Being—you have found a vibrational match and you hold that for 17 seconds, + 17 seconds.

ARE YOU A CREATOR OR REACTOR?

For years, I have shared in classes that when you are frustrated, sad or depressed, you are in a reacting mode, rather than creating. Being a **CREATOR** is deliciously allowing your Stream of Well Being. A **REACTOR** is the same identical letters transposed, which is an energy of resistance or pushing against. It feels like you are stepping on your own hose and pinching off Source. You know instinctively how your energy repels or attracts.

As you become clearer on step two of deliberate creation of what you desire through your emotions, you bring yourself to step three of deliberate creation and find a vibrant vibrational match to what it is that you do want. The things you are saying YES to are excited, luminous energies being launched, propelled and shooting out into the Universe in a powerful fashion which then connect to Source energy! You are a co-creator with the Universe. This is the pure, positive, passionate, pulsating, penetrating energy that creates worlds! This is God Force. This is powerful energy. When you are connected to Source, these luminous, good feeling thoughts are shooting out in a powerful fashion! If you hold that for 17 seconds energetically, an explosion – literally combustion takes place. It is always attracting more of whichever energy wave you are feeding. Relish those good feeeeelings and know emotionally this is where the juice is and milk it for all it's worth!

3) What is the single-most important spiritual practice that promotes peace and prosperity within your own life?

"Joy is the sign that creative emotion is fulfilling its purpose." - Charles Du Bos

My experience has been that there isn't just one single-most spiritual practice when we are constantly evolving and unfolding. However, there are some really wonderful, creative and life changing processes that I love for flowing energy to promote joy, peace and prosperity. I write a monthly column for Arizona Together Newspaper entitled: How Are You Flowing Your Energy? It is posted online monthly at: http://www.magnetizingyourheartsdesire.com

The following is an excerpt from ***Flowing Your Energy***©, June, 2002 in a column about intentions and interfaced with the ***BECAUSE*** process that is very effective:

I CREATE THE JUICE

Think of an hourglass at the midpoint with the upper chamber and neck hovering over your heart's desires as a time continuum that is dropping in your **INTENTIONS** with steady consistency. Your intent's importance, meaning the charge you feeeeel based on your beliefs and your passion for your heart's desire (without resistance), is then determined by how long it takes to be fully released or dissipated in time. You ask and intend, boundaries yield and Source answers when you are aligned with aliveness and focused awareness. Then, a progression of events is pulled into physical reality. Intents cannot shove their way into expression all at one time. They are broken down in a span of time. My February column, ***Being A Drip***, shared how meditations are initially just 'drips.' Gradually, and with practice, the drips become more frequent until there is no gap between drips and water, which eventually form a stream of consciousness.

I invite you to write down **WHY** you chose to receive your heart's desire (you may be surprised how effective this process is). **I choose it because**...**I receive it because**... **I deserve it because...** and to **BE the CAUSE** in your life. Get out your colored markers and make your outcomes vibrant and alive. Make a **SPECTRUM** OF YOUR SELF. Creating a visual collage is very powerful. Be your own magic genie (imagine=I am a genie = your divine creation). Your clarity is what creates your outcomes fulfilled and your wishes granted with divine timing and synchronicity. Decide and intend what you desire and why. There is deliciousness in creating for the sheer pleasure and joyous anticipation of your heart's desires. You then have a time buffer to change it, re-arrange it or fine tune before it manifests. The Law of Attraction always responds to your most dominant vibration. Then, give thanks it is already here, which molds and sets it in place. Appreciation is the fastest tool for personal growth and it is one of the strongest emotions you have as a CREATOR. Stay focused, follow your heart and let your words and feelings be indelibly etched in your heart so your energy is emotionally matching your highest choices. Believe, dream, will and then put it in the hands of God.

Go confidently in the direction of your dreams.
Live the life you've always imagined! - Thoreau

Another effective process I wrote about in my August, 2002 *Flowing Your Energy©* **column includes highlights of how personally enriching** *God Letters* **have been:**

The I'm-possible DREAM

"The future belongs to those who believe in the beauty of their dreams." *Eleanor Roosevelt*

In my book, ***Magnetizing Your Heart's Desire***, I discuss **The I'm Possible Dream**. The journey of staying conscious and aware is truly a hero's journey. Once we awaken to the universal qualities of the Law of Attraction in action, it is not possible to go back to sleep. I appreciate the following quote from Pope John XXIII for it punctuates the importance of flowing energy for all our heart's desire. **The I'm Possible Dream** is ignited when we excitedly remember to visualize, imagine and focus on what we want.

"Consult not your fears but your hopes and your dreams. Think not about your frustrations, but your unfulfilled potential. Concern yourself not with what you tried and failed in, but with what is still possible for you to do."

When my husband requested gift ideas for my birthday, I asked for an Arizona personalized license plate for **CREATOR**. The first tool as a conscious creator is **INTENT**. Intent signals we are passionately focused with laser precision on our heart's desires with pure, positive, pulsating energy. It is a command to the

Universe that old limiting beliefs are being discarded in favor of higher, life-affirming outcomes. I didn't know that the License Bureau actually issues TWO license plates. What a wonderful gift, as now one plate is adorning my car and the other is on my desk. Creator is a wonderful vibrational metaphor and mirror of how we flowing energy.

In May, when my father who is 88, was hospitalized in Michigan, we needed to make arrangements for a nursing home or hospice. The places I visited, which were my highest outcomes, did not have any rooms available and things looked bleak from "outer appearances." As in zero possibility according to their stats! I affirmed that our highest heart's desire was for Rose Arbor or The Springs, which were the finest and highest quality facilities we've ever seen. I stated my intent with clarity and brevity. I then wrote a **Letter to God** without censoring or analyzing any part of it. I let it flow from my heart and pen onto the hotel stationary and gave profound thanks and considered it done.

I felt a strong sixth sense that this would come to pass easily and quickly because our heart's desire at a feeeeling level was so strong. We locked onto Source's satellite signal with laser beam intent. Many times people worry that their prayers or intents won't come to pass.

With any **I'm Possible Dream** laser intent, you must trust and know that what you focus on expands! My Dad was very excited upon hearing what I wrote and I underscored that we all maintain and keep a high, pure, clear intent for this outcome. Within 48 hours, when we arrived at the hospital on Monday morning, my Dad's paperwork was miraculously being signed and he was transferred to Rose Arbor, the most beautiful space anyone could ever imagine. It is so heartwarming to see a state-of-the-art Hospice brimming with loving care and comfort. Dad's large, private room oozed with well being physically, emotionally and spiritually. It was truly amazing grace and co-creating at its finest.

My husband commented on our flight back home to Arizona that even he was astonished at the light speed with which this occurred. Duaine said this has to be one of your grandest wishes granted in the sense that this outcome made such a huge difference to Dad's well being. Dad asked me to tell the Hospice staff about my Letter to God and how this all transpired. He was so happy and beaming with appreciation when we left Kalamazoo.

When I spoke with him the next day, he had been placed in a sling and lowered into a whirlpool and it felt like heaven. He said, "This place is so great, I may just get better." Ironically, he graduated into higher realms four days later. While we did not anticipate this on a linear level, I know Dad's physical vehicle was worn out. His Inner Being was infused with Spirit's ultimate "I'm Possible Mission" making a higher choice.

I find that Letters to God need to be specific. Nothing changes if you are vague—emblazon your heart's desires with simplicity, specificity and clarity. Once your letter is completed, you can later create and expand with **BECAUSE statements** like: **I want it because**...or...because my heart's desire is now fulfilled, this exciting new outcome is vibrating and radiating into my life **because**...

I feel uplifted writing ***Letters to God*** because it is a fresh rocket going off that is launching and magnetizing new deliberate creations and I know I am connected to Source energetically. It is important to find a thought that feels better when in the midst of challenges. Focus on the donut, and not the hole. It will flow if we LET IT IN. Don't tell God "how." Simply know your letter is received. If we focus on "not having" then that also expands exponentially. If you are vibrating blame, anger, frustration or lack, then you are separated from your good and Inner Being.

Once you **ASK,** be prepared to **RECEIVE**.

Feeeeel yourself allowing and receiving your heart's desire so that the Universe and unseen forces of Well Being converge to fulfill your highest outcome. If things are not feeling good in your life, don't focus on negativity. In Abraham-Hicks material entitled: ***Sara, Book 3***, Solomon was asked, "How do we not do that?" His reply, "By not doing that thing that you do that doesn't let well being in. That means don't focus on the exact opposite of your request. You cannot be in the mode of allowing what you DO want, if you are oozing the vibration of what you don't want."

This means focus on what you want and then consider it done. That brings you to vibrational connection with who you really are.

As a young man, Winston Churchill, the British prime minister whose oratory skills became legend, spent three years struggling to complete the eighth grade because he couldn't master English. Ironically, years later, he was asked to address a commencement at Oxford University. The crowd was thrilled with anticipation as Churchill entered carrying his well-known props, a cane, cigar and top hat. As he put his top hat on the podium and removed the cigar from his mouth, he raised himself to his toes and shouted, "Never give up." A few seconds passed and he raised himself once more on his toes and shouted even more emphatically, "NEVER GIVE UP!" Then he picked up his hat, his cane and his cigar and left. That, dear friends, is the essence of…

The I'm possible DREAM…Never EVER give up!

Plant your dreams in God Letters and miracles will grow as you shine on!

Flowing Your Energy©, August, 2002

Male readers who are baseball enthusiasts especially enjoyed the following month's continuation of God Letters entitled: **"Desire, Ask, Believe, Receive"**

In August column, 2002, I shared how I write Letters to God. Shortly afterward, my husband and I were vacationing in San Francisco. The Giants were home playing the Chicago Cubs and Barry Bonds was going for his 600th home run to set a record. While speaking with the hotel manager, he and my husband agreed there was no way tickets were going to be available to that game unless it was through a "scalper." The next morning, I discussed it with Duaine and he confirmed in his mind, "There is no way we will get tickets!" I responded, "Don't you even have any faith that by setting the intention to go to the ballpark, we can manifest tickets?" He said, "Not for this game when Barry Bonds is possibly going to set an elite record."

"God is in the details. (Anonymous)

Unbeknownst to Duaine, I wrote a God Letter, the essence of which said, "Dear God: I know I am wise enough and smart enough to magnetize two affordable tickets to this game. As a Deliberate Creator, I ask you to help manifest two tickets by noon today. In the Stream of Well Being, I joyously receive this heart's desire now. Thank you, God." I considered it a done deal, as I had done my part: I expressed my heart's desire, I asked, I believed and I was eager to receive my highest outcome by noon.

"A single fantasy can transform a million realities."
Maya Angelou

It was a new adventure for us to take the B.A.R.T. (Bay Area Rapid Transit). We got off at Embarcadaro and transferred to the M.U.N.I. to get to the ballpark. There were three men with tickets sitting outside a restaurant. They inquired if we wanted tickets for the ballgame. We responded, "How much? They were scalpers asking $80 apiece for bleacher seats and $500.00 apiece for box seats. We went into the restaurant and struck up a conversation with very nice owners who confirmed their belief that scalpers were the only way we'd get ticket. Their alternate suggestion was to watch the game on their Big Screen TV. Undaunted, I KNEW my prayer was going to be answered in the way I had asked, I just didn't yet know HOW.

At the box office, there was a long serpentine line of 500 people, who had received wristbands early that morning with numbers on them, which was the order for them to stand in line for potential tickets. I asked one of the officials if I could get into that line so if there were any tickets left, I would be close to the box office. He laughed and said, "There is NO WAY any tickets will be left, but go ahead." I didn't pay attention to their reality or detour into any concern of not getting my heart's desire and highest outcome.

The Reader's Digest condensed version is we ended up standing next to a wonderful woman wearing a wristband, who intended to buy four tickets for herself and her family. In the meantime, her husband appeared and had tickets from a woman wearing a wristband, who had just purchased four tickets, but only needed one. Naturally, he acquired the other three and now had extra tickets. Walla! Answered prayer for us! We felt blessed to have magnetized this wonderful couple and had manifested tickets by

11:05 a.m. You can imagine how tickled we were! We ended up with two splendid seats in the shade, something I hadn't thought to ask for in my God Letter. My husband was stunned and so very happy! San Francisco has an awesome ballpark built on the ocean and we had the breeze to our backs and the fragrance of the salt air intermingled with hot dogs and popcorn. I also really liked hearing a female sports announcer. We basked in joy and gratitude with our heart's desire fulfilled. It doesn't get any better than this. Thank you, God!

Woody Allen has aptly said:

80% of SUCCESS IS SIMPLY SHOWING UP!"

We showed up and our wish was granted!

It was a HOME RUN to our answered prayer.

A friend later commented when I was relating this grand outcome, "Did Duaine momentarily forget who he is married to!" He got such a kick out of that remark. It demonstrates when we have faith in our delicious intentions consistently and persistently, we ooze the vibration of Well Being and the Universe delivers. Like attracts like. Statistics are the result of how others are thinking, but they have nothing to do with how we are flowing energy.

When we are connected with Source, choice is our greatest power and ally for our heart's desire. In my book, ***Magnetizing Your Heart's Desire***, these four steps for deliberate creation are succinctly outlined:

1. Identify what you <u>don't</u> want.
    - ❖ Contrast is important for clarity.
2. Feed the energy of what you <u>DO</u> desire.
    - ❖ Flow energy with positive feeeeelings (fun, joy, appreciation, love).
3. Create a vibrational match emotionally through your feeeeelings.
    - ❖ Imagine! Taste it, touch it, see it, feel it, smell it!
4. Then, allow and receive with eagerness and expectation.
    - ❖ Say Yes! Let the Universe deliver—evidence will abound!

What steps are you taking to wholeheartedly make your dreams come true? It's up to YOU! No one can do it for you. Prayer and intent is the breath of your Spirit saying Y.E.S. knowing <u>Y</u>ou <u>E</u>xude <u>S</u>pirit**. Yes! Yes! Yes! You are the Holy Spirit too.**

Remember to plant your dreams and your heart's desires with fervor.

Magic and miracles then flourish, flow and grow.

Flowing Your Energy © September, 2002

In 2004, many people are more aware of what is transpiring in the spiritual film industry that is making inroads mainstream. In our Arizona, there is a phenomenon happening in Tempe with the incredibly powerful and thought-provoking film entitled, ***What The ^%Bleep@*^ Do We Know!*** It has been driven by word of mouth and held over for many months with packed audiences. It is a refreshingly original film that creates a new and level playing field where <u>science and spirituality meet</u>. It moves at light speed into our hearts and brains where quantum physics and metaphysics merge and reflect back infinite possibilities. *What The Bleep* contains a movie with a story that has direct correlation to the documentary interviews that are interspersed throughout the film with 14 top scientists, mystics and visionaries, combined with amazing animation of how all things are inter-connected.

Most of the audience remains in their seats to see the entire credits, stunned by the implications of what they have just viewed, as well as a strong desire to explore a meaty discussion afterward with anyone who attended. Imagine! A film that actually gets us thinking! It hones in spiritually and scientifically on what an infinite universe is contained within each of us. How refreshing to also hear physicists, visionaries and theologians finding common ground.

The most frequently referenced interview in this film is Dr. Joe Dispenza's comments on how he believes we can project our destiny. He shares how he wakes up each morning and deliberately creates his day. Then out of nowhere, little things happen that are unexplainable and he knows they are the process or result of his creation. He explained that the more he does that, the more he builds a neural net in his brain that accepts it is possible that he is actually creating his day. When we take the time to create our day, we are then literally affecting the quantum field of our daily reality.

"An optimist is someone who goes after Moby Dick in a rowboat and takes the tartar sauce with him." Zig Ziglar

In my book, ***Magnetizing Your Heart's Desire***, I write extensively about being a Deliberate Creator. One segment is entitled, "**Reality is a result of your design**." The best-kept secret in the Universe is that we create our reality! However, we do have to consistently practice and imagine how we want it to be. Most people don't take the time to line up the energy by pre-paving intentions. If we want to change what we are living, we have to also change the balance of our thoughts so that our beliefs and desires are deliciously aligned. Often our heart's desires carry a creative, pure, positive vibration, while our beliefs carry a vibration that contradicts our desire (i.e. not feeling good enough or having self-worth issues). By consciously creating our day, we develop vibrational harmony when we positively focus on how we want it to be (while ignoring any habits of thoughts that would oppose it). Our heart's desires are the catalysts for calling forth our creations, as we consciously breathe life into our intentions hourly, daily, weekly.

Recently my friend, Robin Mullin, shared some thoughts from speaker, Phil Cousineau at Inside Edge, an organization that hosts a breakfast meeting weekly in Orange County, Ca. where nationally recognized people of vision share their knowledge and wisdom on human potential, spirituality, and consciousness. She knows how much I appreciate these kind of inspirational offerings. His new book, *The Olympic Odyssey: Rekindling The True Spirit of the Great Games,* is based on extensive research in the history of sports and the connecting link to mind and spirit. The phrase, ***seize the day*** is actually only half the original sentence by Horus. It originally was: **"Seize the day. Let us sport while we may."** The root of the word ***sport*** means, "being carried away."

Cousineau feels sports are meant to create the experience of feeling that larger connection beyond the physical (in other words, potentially becoming a meta-physical experience). He shared that Franklin D. Roosevelt always read the sports page first to be reminded of man's (woman's) victories and only afterward would FDR then read the front page news about man's difficulties. Recent studies by the University of Minnesota the past several years found that 83% of American kids drop out of sports by the age of 12. The research and reasons given were: 1. Somebody shamed them. 2. It isn't fun anymore, with too much pressure to win/work. 3. Don't play often enough.

It is a fascinating analogy to compare that research to personal reasons given by people for not creating a day the way they want it to be as Deliberate Creators. Reasons could include some of the same elements: **1. Someone shamed them** (i.e. "Who do you think you are?!"), **2. It isn't fun anymore** (i.e. focusing on what didn't work, or being a 'reactor' pushing against rather than a 'creator' moving toward imagined outcomes, and feeeeeling good and excited our heart's desires for the sheer joy and fun of it; **3. Don't play often enough** (not practicing regularly or monitoring thoughts to stay consistently focused on delicious heart's desires so they become a predominant habit of focused vibration). **PLAY** is an important and fun energy for creating all our heart's desires.

"Citius, Altius, Fortius." Faster, Higher, Stronger!
- Olympic quote

Most people are familiar with the power of "**AS IF**" as an approach to life. Acting ***AS IF*** in our imagination cultivates habit patterns and neural networks in our brain forging new possibilities and potential---faster, higher, and stronger. We become what we consistently imagine by holding the vision for our highest outcomes. This goes beyond positive thinking or affirmations because we are lining up the energy for our heart's desires by imprinting our intentions deliberately, consciously and consistently. It is our aligned vibration that emanates from us and locks onto our signal of Well-Being to the Universe.

Our quantum leaps come when we understand we are the creator and the attractor. We simply have to be aware and ask: "Which thought feels better?!" We set our tone and create our day by always knowing what feeeeeels good and what resonates positively within us. The Universe then responds to the vibration we offer. No matter how negative we may feel sometimes, there is no shortage of our highest outcomes being fulfilled as we re-align, re-

remember, practice and focus consciously and vibrantly! Be bold—go for the gold in the game of life—get carried away! All of the processes described in this segment have been personally life changing and empowering. When you need a fresh start, always come from your heart and do what feels good!

4) Imagine you are having a conversation with God (or the Universal creator or whatever name you prefer)... Share with us what is being said about the scope and future of Spirituality in the Entrepreneurial Business world.

Your Life is in Your Hands

There is a beautiful Indian story about a Master who lived in the Himalayas and the children of the village wanted to outsmart him. So they decided to fool the Master by having one of the children hold a bird behind his back in his hands. They would then ask, "Master is the bird dead or alive?" If the Master said, "The bird is alive," they would then wring the bird's neck to make the Master wrong. If the Master said, "The bird is dead," then they would let the bird live and the Master would be wrong. Either way, the children figured he would look foolish and the children would be pleased to have outwitted him.

So, they went to this wise old Master and said, "Master, what do we have in these hands?" He replied, "A bird." They asked, "Is it dead or alive?"
And he replied, "**It's in your hands.**"

Your life is in your hands. It always has been and always will be. Ultimately, who you are really matters only to you. As an entrepreneur, let your spirit expand, be willing, enthusiastic and excited in all life's adventures, initiatives and undertakings by asking:

- What is my highest passion now?
- What makes my heart sing and my soul soar?
- Where am I most divinely enthusiastic at this time?
- What thrills and fulfills me?
- What is fun, joyful and exhilarating?
- What feeds and nourishes me?
- What animates my vision for inspired decisions?

- What sparkles in my soul that is seeking to express and bless?

You are a Deliberate Creator through your expectations and eagerness to flow energy. Be resourceful, bodacious and bold as you go for the gold. Who you are is a direct result of your thoughts, feelings and vibration as a Deliberate Creator. Ultimately, you have only you to depend upon. All energy follows thought. Love what you are, invest in yourself and let your light SHINE as a person, an entrepreneur, and a co-creator pulsating, radiating, vibrating and following your bliss to manifest magnetize your heart's desire! Begin now! Appreciate and celebrate yourself and your entrepreneurial spirit!

* * * * * * * *

Sharon A. Warren, M.A., Amazing Grace Unlimited, Chandler, Arizona

Submitted by: Sharon A. Warren, M.A. (Author), Amazing Grace Unlimited,
Phone: 480 816-9930 e-mail: iam@amazinggracenow.com

Hard Bound Book:
Magnetizing Your Heart's Desire - $22.
ISBN: 0967499011
Includes a set of rare-earth magnets
E-book: *Magnetizing Your Heart's Desire* - $19.95
Magnets are not included. Can be ordered separately for $ **5.**
http://www.magnetizingyourheartsdesire.com (columns)
http://www.lawofattractioninaction.com
http://leadingedgecreators.com
Author's Talking Web sites: **http://www.amazinggracenow.com (orders)**

"If you start to think the problem is 'out there,' stop yourself. That thought is the problem."
-- Stephen Covey

Larry Wayne

1) New information reveals that 75%+ of the world's most successful people are profoundly spiritual in both belief and practice. Describe how your personal and business success has evolved through Spiritual Influences.

The heart and soul of Spiritual Influences is: love – compassion – gentleness – kindness – understanding. Love was the answer to all problems; it was the miracle cure, the wonder drug of our future.

Love is our purpose and mission in life, and we had to learn to love ourselves first, so we could give the gifts we had to offer the world.

People are trying to love what they do, but fail to love what they are. If they loved themselves first that love will flow into the work and all will be successful i.e.: love what you do and you share with the world. Love what you are and you grow and expand.

Love is the passion, the power you have for yourself and for what you do

---

If you feel and accept the unconditional love from your own indwelling spirit, your negative conditions and humanness are washed away forever, leaving you whole and pure. Why not let the love in, which makes you worthy, forget the human conditions and simply make a choice.

The realization of unconditional love will move you into magic and miracles; no one else can give that to you, but you.

Put as much effort into being powerful, wealthy and wise, as you do in loving that special someone in your life.

L – O – V – E when you spell it – means – LIGHT OF VICTORY EVERYWHERE!

2) In what ways do you incorporate your Spiritual Beliefs into day-to-day business interactions?

<u>In A Lot Of Ways – Life Is Like A Menu:</u>

***Appetizers*:** True knowledge – some say knowledge is power but that is not true. Knowledge leads you into the power, the power gives you knowledge i.e.: being in the "zone" means super conscious spirit gives you the answers and solutions. If you have the answers to your questions and the solutions to your problems you don't have any problems.

Negative problems don't mean anything if you find the answers and solutions. Do you know why you can find the answers and solutions? Because you are the answer and resolution – one source provides all.

Entrée: The awakened perspective, which is an awareness of your potentially and powers. The awakened perspective is so important. You are in this world but not of it. You are not your past. You are not your physical body. You are such stuff that dreams are made of! i.e.: you are greater than any problem.

P – O – W – E – R – which when you spell it means personal oneness within every reality. Power is of the mind, your mind and understanding the needs of others. Power is in your knowledge, which can be expanded into more. Power is in your talents, gifts and abilities of the spirit, which you carry within you.

Enlightenment is being and expressing the elements of love, positivity, confidence which are emotions and energies that make up a force, a power.

Being enlightened means, being able to change the negatives and find the positives. Work through problems and resolve issues. Use the power of love and release negative ego.

Desert: Truth and wisdom, which is the "How To", like the owner's manual; it reveals how your choice can be expanded into more. i.e.: into multiple streams of plenty and prosperity, richness, happiness, winning and success.

Drinks: Light and purge positive energy, which aids in the assimilation of goodness and greatness, mystery and magic, which holds no impossibilities, everything and anything can happen. It is imagination and fantasy made real.

3) What is the single-most important spiritual practice that promotes peace and prosperity within your own life?

Controlling the mind, determining what is, being spirit in action.

All you humanly are is mind, choice. Whatever you put into that mind is personal, that is what makes you different, individual, unique. What is the common denominator between human and spirit? Mind, yet, different through choices. The only permanency is mind. All you are is mind, which can take form. i.e.: human, spirit, light.

Powerful people are simply making powerful choices

All the human must be, is the choice, the human must simply choose more and accept more. Accept the power is there, ready to create any choice you make. i.e.: don't focus on making the human more, make the choice more. Choose and then decide it is, that is the key.

You are the power behind the thoughts. You are not what others made you – you are what you have decided to be. The energies, which are the raw material of creation, are not affected by other people by chance, but by choice. i.e.: choice is the most significant talent you have. Tell the power or, pre-programmed energies that you want and lit it work for you.

4) Imagine you are having a conversation with God (or the Universal creator or whatever name you prefer)... Share with us what is being said about the scope and future of Spirituality in the Entrepreneurial Business world.

You are here incognito as a human male or female: you play that role but you are spirit. It is time to drop your disguise and be all that you are. You have learned the life as human, now you become your true self in the same lifetime; that is a great accomplishment.

This is extremely rare because most people don't become the spirit being in their lifetime. i.e.: if you will not be all you are, how do you expect to get all you need?

There are two reasons to be centered in power and wisdom

The need of the human to know it's powers; to see, feel and experience it.

To utilize the power and wisdom to be spirit, the talent, gift, ability and to create; to be, do and have whatever you truly need and desire.

The new philosophy of successful,
wealthy people is that you create your own reality

You have the power to make any choice your reality. You are not your human mass conscious thoughts, emotions, actions – that is passé, that does not fit into the lifestyle of who you are now! i.e.: you have one thing that will keep you interested and that is you, and not as a being who uses power, but as a being who is power.

Man seeks the power and looks everywhere for it while it resides within each and everyone. When there are no more places to look – or – when life has become unbearable he eventually turns inward. It is there his journey begins and sometimes its arduous and painful but eventually he learns who and what he is and then he can determine the rest of the journey. He can then relax and enjoy the journey knowing he controls the outcome and so controls its destiny.

Sometimes it takes many years to come to this understanding but the results in reaching this stage far exceeds the journey never taken.

5) What hasn't been asked that should have been addressed or answered?

An important question to ask yourself:

What is the most difficult thing for you to take into the human mind, that spirit self possess? i.e.: it is love, self love, self value, confidence or inner trust, making a stand for yourself in the creation of your own true reality, or truth? Then you will know what you need.

There is one particular purpose in life.
To find it look at your greatest need

Ask yourself, what is the one thing you have been searching for that has been illusive? What is the one thing you have wanted more than anything? It may be "love" your true purpose and mission in life!

When you love yourself, you value all the talents, gifts, abilities within and love releases, activates and amplifies them, and brings them forward in literal action for you to display what you are. The power you have is love.

You must love the choices you make, so they will manifest

Start each choice with love; add the element of love to all your goals. This activates the pre-programmed energies, to manifest success in all that you do and are. i.e.: goals don't give you love, but will give you goals.

If you act loving or do loving things before you are love, then the act of love is just that, an act. i.e.: it is the humanistic patterns of do and give to receive, and you must be able to receive. You can't teach people to love, but what you can do is show them it is safe to love, and the natural or true emotion comes forward.

> Love is the light for truth – truth is light but you control the amount of light that you will give to your truth. i.e.: you are not here to love the world, you are here to be in the world, that is powerful that is wisdom.

* * * * * * * *

Larry Wayne is a pioneer in the field of realizing who you are, and creating what you truly want.

Call Larry at 403-228-0300 for your free 11 Keys to Miraculous Success
Or visit http://www.LivingInPowerAndWisdom.com

"Our business in life is not to get ahead of others, but to get ahead of ourselves - to break our own records, to outstrip our yesterday by our today."-- Stewart B. Johnson

---

Troy White

1) New information reveals that 75%+ of the world's most successful people are profoundly spiritual in both belief and practice. Describe how your personal and business success has evolved through Spiritual Influences.

In my past I had always been one to shun spirituality as I thought it meant religion. From what I saw of the mess that the various religious groups were in, I wanted nothing of it.

When I learned the big difference between the two, my life changed.

3 years ago I could not even spell spirituality!

I found a wonderful book that started my evolution and education on what spirituality is and what it means, how to use spiritual beliefs and practice to grow as a person. "The Artists Way" by Julia Cameron is that book and it taught me how to get back in touch with the true essence of Troy and who he really is.

Since working with that book, I am now a co-author of a #1 best selling book. I have been self employed successfully now for almost 3 years (at time of this), my rates have tripled over the past 12 months, have held numerous successful seminars, have grown an incredible network of business associates (as you can see in this book), survived the first 4 years of having twin daughters, kept semi-sane with both my wonderfully supporting wife Kari and I working out of the home, and am more at peace with who I really am than ever before.

I don't repeat any of this to boast but to show what can be accomplished in a very short period of time when the spiritual side of you is awakened.

What is most amazing to me about spirituality is that despite what science now proves as fact with the "other side" of life many people still have a tough time accepting that it is possible and that it is reality.

Mankind has one heck of an ego!

Despite all the scientific facts showing that what we truly know (which is not much) about ourselves, about the universe, and about the energy field that surrounds us, many people still think they know it all.

What has been one of the greatest realizations in my journey is that we still know very little about ourselves and what makes up "us and the universe". Every day that changes though, new research findings comes out, people are more willing to talk about their spiritual side, the proof being all around us, and a general awakening is now inevitable.

What it means to you is that a deeper understanding of spirituality, how your spirit impacts your life, and how you can awaken your inner self, are all very much within your grasp today.

This book has an enormous amount of information and tips you can use to get in touch with your higher self – and use that connection to reach the levels of success you truly desire.

2) In what ways do you incorporate your Spiritual Beliefs into day-to-day business interactions?

It has taken me some time to find what works best for me. And I think it's only possible to discover this through trial and error to find what resonates and works best with you. Also, part of the reason I asked so many people to contribute to this book is that I knew, from my own experience, that one technique does not work for everyone.

I've tried; journaling, affirmations, subliminal work, music, meditation, spiritual coaching, reiki, hypnotherapy, workbooks, classes, courses, visualizations, goal setting, breathing exercises – to name just a few.

What is working best for me right now is a combination of the following.

Feeling gratitude to all that which is good around me – keeping a daily log of things that happen to me during the day that make me feel good, or when money comes into my life through unexpected sources. I find that just writing down all the incredible people, resources, and opportunities in my life via the written form attracts more of what I pay attention to

Magical money journal – the universe loves positive energy and feelings around things so I now spend $1,000, $10,000, even $100,000 per day (on paper). I get myself in "shopping mode" and spend the money every day. Some days I give the money to worthy causes. Other days I buy "toys". The universe and your subconscious mind cannot tell what is real – only what is positive energy around you. So when you spend money happily every day on paper you are telling the universe and your subconscious mind that you are comfortable spending it and feel positive emotions while around money. This is highly effective! Michael Losier of the book The Law of Attraction taught me this and it is VERY powerful.

Meditation – I was fortunate to also discover Centerpointe at http://www.getspiritual.com/meditation.htm early on and found that their programs provide rapid results in meditation and in self-growth. While I don't use this technology every day, I do find some way (at least once a day) to quiet the mind and put myself in the flow of true silence. If you do not meditate now – get on it! It is the most incredible tool in my eyes for dealing with stress, challenges, ideas etc. Centerpointe is an excellent place to start. http://www.getspiritual.com/meditation.htm

> **Side note**: Many of my most profitable ideas have come to me while meditating. When you quiet your conscious mind, amazing things happen in the background in your subconscious mind and it spits out some incredible ideas. Keep a pen and paper near you at all times for those "ideas from out of the blue".

Visualization – key for me to imagine in as much detail as possible what my dream life looks like, feels like, smells like, tastes like etc. I have pictures up on my wall of my dream house, dream car, dream boat, etc. I look at them for five minutes or so then close my eyes and imagine myself enjoying all that which I truly desire.

Remember – the universe and the subconscious mind cannot tell what is real and what is imagined with emotion – so put your all into your visualizations – imagine what it really feels like to drive the car of your dreams, earning the income your have always wanted, taking the vacations you always dreamed of, the relationships you have always desire.

Get into it and really feeeeeeel what it is like.

Journaling is an excellent tool to manifest things in your life. I got started three years ago and to this day I still find it very relaxing, releasing and incredibly powerful in what you can create while sketching it out on paper. Journal on where you are going… write about what it looks like, feels like, smells like etc. Write about all that you do on an average day when you reach your dream life. Write about all the positive people and relationships you have in your life. Write about all the people you help along the way. Write about what you will do when money flowing in a constant stream. Write about anything and everything that makes you feel powerful.

Determining exactly what it is that I want in my life today, tomorrow and a year from now. By making the choice that I want four new clients in the month of January for example and making sure the universe knows I am serious about it (through the emotions I feel when I think about it)… I almost always get it.

Discovering and feeling the power center of my heart. This one is a tough one. Tough to talk about and tough to explain. I have never really shared this anywhere else but this would be the best place of them all. When I am really in the flow and feeling good about my life, my relationships, my success, and my future – my heart feels like it is on fire! I can feel the energy being raised as I type this and I know that I am vibrating on an entirely new level.

Best way I can describe it is for you to recall that feeling of being deeply in love. That feeling resides around your heart – and that is a VERY powerful feeling. Imagine living life with your heart feeling like that 24/7. This takes work, and as all parts of life, has its ups and downs. But once you understand the power that lies within your heart – you will always be working to bring back that feeling.

An amazing thing you will discover – when that feeling is there at full flow and energy – amazing things will happen in your life – I guarantee it. Work on bringing that feeling forward on command – it will create miracles.

3) What is the single-most important spiritual practice that promotes peace and prosperity within your own life?

Definitely meditation for peace and stress-free living. While some days I have to force myself to take the time for meditation – I always feel a million times better after. It is absolutely amazing how rested you can feel after 30 minutes of a quiet mind. If you have never meditated before, I highly encourage you to start now and use tools like Centerpointe to get yourself going.

http://www.getspiritual.com/meditation.htm

The second practice that has helped me immensely is a gratitude journal, combined with the magical money journal. In the short time I have been using those tools, I have manifested some great things in my life and you will too.

The last thing that I will encourage you to use is your intuition, or gut feeling. It almost never fails you. A large majority of CEO's use their intuition to make major business decisions; if it doesn't feel right – it doesn't happen.

My intuition has warned me about three companies in advance. When I used to work for others in the computer world, three times I just had "a feeling" that it was time to move on and I did. And two of those three times, the company ended up being bankrupt in six months or less. And the third time, they didn't go bankrupt but it was the last time my intuition had to tell me to leave and go work for myself.

I listened. I followed. And I love it!

4) Imagine you are having a conversation with God (or the Universal creator or whatever name you prefer)... Share with us what is being said about the scope and future of Spirituality in the Entrepreneurial Business world.

Many successful business owners today are highly spiritual and are big believers that they can control their future and success with the power of the universe at your side. We are reaching a point now where people are more open to spiritual practices as science is finally giving us proof that it works. And people need proof so the scientific facts are encouraging many people to consider things, which they never would have considered before.

What is about to happen is a complete shift in thinking in the way we live our lives. The movie "What The Bleep Do We Know?" has caught a lot of attention and people are taking note. We <u>want</u> to know more about spirituality and how we can control our future.

There is coming a time, not so far from now, when people will use mediation, visualization and many other spiritual practices, to create everything they have ever desired.

Business owners will consult their own "knowing" before making decisions. Intuition skills will be taught in business schools as an instrumental way to make decisions (64% of the most successful business leaders use intuition as the driving force in their decision making – that will be 100% soon).

Visualization will be encouraged in schools starting from kindergarten and the antiquated school systems will realize that the mind training curriculum's are priority #1.

This will raise a generation of adults that are 100% in control of their thoughts, and their manifestations.

Imagine an entire generation of entrepreneurs that can create success, partnerships, profits, and highly satisfied clients with relative ease.

Business start-ups will be much easier to make succeed. Competitiveness will reach a level that encourages working together as one on profitable partnerships.

5) What hasn't been asked that should have been addressed or answered?

Why is it that spirituality is still something that many are scared to discuss? Many of the most successful business people in the world are highly spiritual – yet they don't like to talk about it. There is a mass confusion and fear out there that still controls us all.

Be the one that breaks free from what the masses say. The masses do not live their lives full of health, happiness, abundance or joy. So listening to them is not a very solid path to living a successful life, is it?

Live life on your own terms, listen to your heart and your intuition and they will steer you in the right directions. It may seem like a strange path they lead you on at first but the day will come when it is all laid out before you and it will seem so obvious why this path was the one you went down.

And when that day comes, you will see things with crystal clear vision that makes all things easily within your grasp.

The reason why this subject is still relatively tough to discuss with many people is that they are scared that it might be true.

Imagine what a world it would be if you were totally in control of everything that happened to you.

Everything you thought of came true – positive or negative.

A world where you could no longer blame others, or the situation for what you have in your life.

A world that is all interconnected by an invisible force.

An invisible force that you can control.

A world that is completely open to abundance, prosperity and wealth – in fact - the world is full of abundance, prosperity and wealth – poverty is cause by close minded (and negative) thinking.

To me, this is exciting and something I am striving to master.

To others, that is a scary world that they can't see – and if you can't see it, it mustn't exist.

To you, the world is in your hands and the tools in this book will take you well on your way to accomplishing anything and everything you could possibly imagine.

Dream big.

Make your future all that you could ever desire and then please pass on your successful ideas and techniques to others who want to learn to control their reality.

To your massive success!

* * * * * * * *

Troy White
"Turning Your Words Into Wealth"
http://www.SmallBusinessCopywriter.com
http://www.MarketingESP.com
http://www.CalgaryAdClinic.com
403.259.4566
troy@entrepeneurialspirits.com

"If you're prosperous in soul, you'll be prosperous in whole."
-- Mark Victor Hansen

Warren Whitlock

1) New information reveals that 75%+ of the world's most successful people are profoundly spiritual in both belief and practice. Describe how your personal and business success has evolved through Spiritual Influences.

I generally find it hard to describe the spiritual influence in my business life for two reasons. First, I can't imagine doing anything in life that was "separate" from my spirit, and second, in business, it's generally considered taboo to discuss spiritual or religious values.

There is no way I can make it to the next breath, let alone through a business day, with my spirit. I'm reminded of the phrase "all things are spiritual unto God" and have reflected on this many times. How could God do anything that wasn't spiritual? And if that were so, how would I dare consider it?

Most successful people I know are extremely well balanced. In fact, that's what success is to me. So it stands to reason that they would be spiritual.

I think anyone saying that they are "non-spiritual" is deluding themselves or just blind to the obvious.

There are many things I don't understand about the universe, which sort of proves the point that there are forces out there that aren't physical.

As for the "taboo", maybe it's generally a good idea. To focus on spiritual in business can sometime move the discussion off the urgent matters at hand. Business is getting things done, and outward spirituality can divert the discussion. But every day, in every activity, I feel the influence of a greater power. When I listen to these prompting, business goes better.

2) In what ways do you incorporate your Spiritual Beliefs into day-to-day business interactions?

My values are God and Family first but God doesn't want me idle, and my family likes to eat.

As long as you have your priorities straight, God wants you to prosper.

I pray every day for business success so that I might do more good in this world for God and His children.

3) What is the single-most important spiritual practice that promotes peace and prosperity within your own life?

Prayer and meditation.

4) Imagine you are having a conversation with God (or the Universal creator or whatever name you prefer)... Share with us what is being said about the scope and future of Spirituality in the Entrepreneurial Business world.

I do have an ongoing conversation with God, (some would call that prayer). I'm constantly asking for peace, and inquiring how I may serve.

* * * * * * * *

Warren Whitlock
The Marketing Results Coach

http://www.marketingresultscoach.com/

"If we plant a seed in the ground we know that the sun will shine and the rain will water, and we leave it to the Law to bring results... Well, the desire you image is the seed, your occasional closing of the eyes in imagery is the sun, and your constant, though not anxious, expectation is the rain and cultivation necessary to bring absolutely sure results..."-- Frances Larimer Warner

---

Judy Wilkie

1) Describe how my personal and business success has evolved through spiritual influences:

My personal and business success has evolved beyond my wildest dreams as a result of spiritual practices. I understand I create my own reality and by setting intentions, loving what I do, being passionate, creative, kind receptive and open to expansiveness I create abundance and joy in my life. By operating from principles of patience, peace, harmony and joy, life is easy and fun and fulfilling.

2) In what way do I incorporate my spiritual belief's into day to day business interactions.

I incorporate my spiritual belief's into day to day business through every thought, emotion and action I think, feel or do.

3) What is the single most important spiritual practice that promotes peace and prosperity in my life?

I would say without a doubt meditation. Meditation allows me to make conscious contact with the source, God, God is all there is. In making that contact, the power of intention is intensified, my thoughts are loving and peaceful, my emotions are in harmony with all that is and my actions show are wise and powerful.

4) Imagine a conversation with God. What is being said about the scope and future of spirituality in the entrepreneurial business world.

To me God is all the elements of love. A gentle powerful flowing loving force. God would say, there simply is no other way to operate if you desire the results you are asking for. Simply put, you have genius in you, you have pure potential, use it by giving, being kind, loving and generous and all will be yours.

Intend and it is.

Desire and it is. Focus on what you intend and desire and it will be. It is all that simple. Every thought, emotion and action must be congruent. Do not doubt or fear or you will lose your way.

* * * * * * * *

Judy Wilkie
http://www.spiritofmarriage.com – 39 minutes to stress free wedding
http://www.theweddingblueprint.com – all your wedding plans done in an afternoon!

"No one succeeds without effort ... Those who succeed owe their success to their perseverance." - Ramana Maharshi

Ralph Zuranski

1) New information reveals that 75%+ of the world's most successful people are profoundly spiritual in both belief and practice. Describe how your personal and business success has evolved through Spiritual Influences.

My spiritual beliefs contribute greatly to my physical and emotional health, financial success and daily enjoyment of life. As powerful events catapult me down the mysterious pathways of life, my relationship with God is a wellspring of strength, a reservoir of hope and the foundation of my moral code.

Recent events had a huge impact on my perspective and what is important in life. In the blink of an eye, my life changed permanently. My mom came down with congestive heart failure in March. On Sunday, May 23, 2004 my dad suffered a catastrophic stroke.

Before this occurred, everything was going according to my schedule. I was attending Internet Marketing Conferences, searching for "Internet Heroes" to help with my "In Search Of Heroes Copywriting Program for High School Journalism and Multi-media Students." My goal was to spread good news about local heroes through a grassroots effort by high school journalists.

To pay my way, I shot professional photos of speakers and attendees, ran the PowerPoint presentations and created theme websites for each event. Life was very good.

Words cannot describe my emotions when my parents were near death. When both of them were struck down, within 90 days of each other, the stress is unimaginable. Your heart drops into the pit of your stomach. Indecision plagues your footsteps. You just do not know what to do.

Everyone has times of great joy and sorrow. It is a natural part of life. Trials and tribulations affect all of our lives. How we deal with catastrophes and even minor irritants determines our ultimate happiness and success.

When trials and tribulations intrude into our daily lives, fear increases. Our peace decreases. With both of my parents suffering catastrophic health events, my only real defense against fear, anger, depression, despair and indecision was prayer and choosing a positive attitude.

When catastrophic events impact our lives, we realize how little control we really exert over daily events. In times of crisis, trusting totally in God's goodness is a useful defense against the destructive thought processes that cripple our ability to be healthy, productive individuals.

Often, there is very little we can do to change any of the outcomes that are beyond our control. A tremendous amount of stress is removed when we trust in God and realize everything is in His capable hands. All we can do is pray and help out where needed.

Physical disease, injuries, financial failure and family problems teach us important lessons about God's love, mercy, forgiveness and grace. Healing in all areas of life can signify a positive transformation of our relationship with God. Doctors and psychologists still cannot explain the beneficial impact of prayer and faith.

Personal health challenges and catastrophic injuries or disease that affect our loved ones can do more to improve or destroy our relationship with God than just about anything! Our battles with pain, illness, injuries, financial difficulties and family problems are waged on emotional, physical, intellectual and spiritual levels. Our emotional roller coaster, because of what is happening in our lives, is a daily battle against depression, fear, desperation and despair.

Seeking a healthy relationship with Jesus is one of the major factors of my success in overcoming the tragedies in my life. Once I established a personal relationship with Jesus, it gave me the faith, trust and optimism necessary to have victory over the major and minor challenges.

The catastrophic illness of my parents has only been the latest and greatest personal challenge. For my entire life I have battled sickness, pain and negative emotions. When I could go no further, I discovered the spirit of God is stronger than the flesh. Through His strength anything is possible.

My life-long battle for physical, emotional and financial health and a pain-free existence has been a real challenge. Fighting to overcome poor health, hormonal imbalances, chronic pain, severe injuries and depression was not easy.

Sometimes it felt like I was drowning in a sea of despair. I have no doubt my physical and mental health would be only a lost memory, if not for my relationship with Jesus.

Long ago, I learned that the love of money, power, sex, material possessions and selfishness does not lead to happiness. For many years, I turned away from my Christian upbringing then I discovered the truth. "There is a way that seems right to man, but that path is the way of death, destruction and unhappiness."

The primary message of Jesus was LOVE. "Love your enemies, do good to those who hate you. Bless those that curse you. Pray for those who despitefully use and persecute you. The only way to overcome is evil is with good."

Jesus was always talking about loving your neighbour and laying your life down for a friend. He even tells us to feed our enemy if he is hungry. Give him drink if he is thirsty.

It is difficult to turn your cheek when someone offends you. Loving your neighbour as yourself is hard. Considering others more valuable is no 'walk in the park.' Giving to the poor, helping the sick and visiting the imprisoned definitely infringes on the hours I could be making money.

We can become living examples of God's mercy and compassion, regardless of our faith or religious denomination. More people like Mother Theresa and Gandhi are desperately needed in the world today.

I am very thankful for the free gift of salvation. It is not based on my works, but on the personal sacrifice of Jesus Christ. It is not earned or deserved. This free gift can never be lost.

Any good we do is not because we are trying to gain anything. We seek to live exceptional lives of service out of gratitude for what Jesus did for us.

What a sobering thought it is when you realize you are a sinner who deserves to pay for your sins. I am one of the most grateful people you will ever meet. My ability to successfully deal with the current sorrows and difficulties in my life is directly related to the power of the Holy Spirit.

Once the teachings of Christ actually began to make sense, my life and health gradually transformed. Until then, the bible was meaningless, a book that was far more infuriating than enlightening.

Fortunately there is hope for the future. No matter the size of the problems now facing you and your family, there are spiritual heroes and heroines everywhere. They are willing to inspire others by helping graciously without expecting anything in return.

I have come to the realization that my purpose on earth is to minister to each person God puts on my path in a positive way. Ultimately, people are the most valuable. Nothing compares to the joy of helping others.

Hopefully, when I pass from this world and enter heaven, Jesus will say to me, "Well done, good and faithful servant!"

2) In what ways do you incorporate your Spiritual Beliefs into day-to-day business interactions?

My spiritual beliefs guide my daily actions. I spend at least an hour praying every morning. I say the rosary. Then I ask for God's blessings on family members and hundreds of friends and business associates.

My goal is to follow God's plan for my life rather than my own. Sometimes it is not easy to "Trust in the Lord with all your heart.

Lean not to your own understanding. Acknowledge Him in all your ways and let Him direct your paths."

Below is my daily prayer that includes numerous positive affirmations with the condition that following God's will triumphs over my own desires.

I, Ralph Zuranski, am a person of integrity. I have a good attitude. My goals are very specific. I have a high energy level, am enthusiastic, and take pride in my appearance and what I do. I have a sense of humor, lots of faith, wisdom and the vision, empathy and courage to use my talents effectively.

I have character and am knowledgeable. My convictions are strong. I have a healthy self-image, a passion for what is right, and a solid hope for the future.

I am fully equipped for the Divine plan for my life. God is my unfailing supply.

Every plan my Father in heaven has not planned shall be dissolved and dissipated. His Divine Will now comes to pass.

Only that which is true of God is true for me. As I am one with God through the indwelling of the Holy Spirit. I am blessed by God's goodness.

Divine Love now dissolves and dissipates every wrong conditioning of my mind, body and affairs. Divine Love is the most powerful force in the universe. It eliminates everything that is not truly of God. Divine Love fills my consciousness with peace, health, life, joy and anticipation of being with the Lord forever.

My eyes are God's eyes. I see with the eyes of the Spirit. I see clearly the open way. There are no obstacles on my pathway. I see clearly the perfect plan.

I am divinely sensitive to my intuitive leads and give instant obedience to God's will.

I cast all my burdens on Jesus Christ and I go free.

I am an honest, sincere, hard-working person. I am tough but fair and sensitive. I'm disciplined, motivated, and focused. I am a good listener and patient, but take decisive action. I am bold and confident, yet humble.

I am an encourager, a restorer and a forgiving person. I am caring, unselfish and committed. I am family-oriented, open-minded and an excellent communicator.

I am a student, a teacher and a self-starter. I am obedient, loyal, responsible and dependable. I have a servant's heart, am ambitious and a team player. I am personable, optimistic and organized. I am resourceful, intelligent, competent, persistent and creative. I am health-conscious, balanced and clean. I am flexible, punctual and thrifty. I am healthy and my entire body with every cell healed and strong.

I am an honorable person who is truly grateful for the opportunity life has given me. These are the qualities of the winner I was born to be and I fully intend to develop these marvellous qualities with which I have been entrusted.

Faith is the substance of things hoped for, the evidence of things not seen for faith holds the vision steady. Adverse pictures are dissolved and dissipated. In due season I will reap what I have sown, if I persevere to the end and faint not. We are under grace, not law. The gifts of God are poured out on me. Jesus has overcome the world. Be of good cheer.

What can I do to become a better ambassador of God today and be a better witness for Jesus Christ?
How can I be a better husband and grandpa?
How can I become healthier physically today?
How can I be a more loving and kind person?
How can I be more successful in business?

Tonight I'm going to sleep wonderfully well. I will dream powerful, positive dreams. I will awaken energized and refreshed. Tomorrow's going to be magnificent.

These are the qualities of the winner I was born to be. Today is the first day of the rest of my life, and it is wonderful.

3) What is the single-most important spiritual practice that promotes peace and prosperity within your own life?

Daily prayer and meditation on God's goodness is important. By following His laws and studying the wisdom contained in the bible it is easier to align my decisions with His master plan for my life. If I abide by His laws and follow His suggestions, my peace and happiness is insured no matter what is going on in my life.

4) Imagine you are have a conversation with God (or the Universal creator or whatever name you prefer)... Share with us what is being said about the scope and future of Spirituality in the Entrepreneurial Business world.

Well Jesus, I used to focus on what I wanted. It was easy to view everyone else as totally screwed up. I saw their failings and insufficiencies. Everyone else was to blame for my mistakes and failings, but not me.

I gloried in my own strength and wisdom. My physical prowess was legendary. Then, you showed me the truth through personal trials and tribulations.

My personal suffering was required to stop trusting in myself. It was not until you allowed me to personally experience the extremes of weakness, the power of fear and depths of sorrow that I learned your plan for my life.

Life is not about serving self and building up wealth and accumulating material possessions. When I came to realize that people are the primary source of happiness and sorrow in my life, my eyes were opened.

The greatest act we can do it spreading your love one person at a time. Serving others without expectation of rewards is truly the pathway to happiness.

If only the world would not have to go through the pain and suffering I have experienced. But, I guess most people are just like me.

As long as we have an abundant supply of money, material possessions and health without spiritual discernment, the experience of true peace and unshakable joy is only a glimmer of what is possible.

Please have mercy on everyone else. Perhaps they won't have to suffer as much as I have to experience the great joy and peace that goes beyond understanding.

5) What hasn't been asked that should have been addressed or answered?

Who are the individuals that are the unsung spiritual heroes in the world?

The saviours of humanity are young people, parents, grandparents, neighbours, teachers, coaches and individuals who demonstrate true unconditional love. They invest their time, energy and resources to help others. They are constantly working to make the world a better place, without expecting payment or even recognition. These individuals are the role models the world needs now.

* * * * * * * *

Ralph Zuranski
3639 Midway Dr. Ste. B299
San Diego, CA 92110
619-990-9492
E-mail: Biomans@bigfoot.com
http://www.InSearchOfHeroes.com
http://www.PolishPower.com
http://www.HealthyDoctors.com

Who is this Troy White Guy?

Troy is President and Founder of the Fresh Idea Company and is an internationally known expert in Turning Your Words Into Wealth. If you own your own business (or are planning to) then the ability to market yourself and your business is critically important.

From direct mail sales letters, postcard campaigns, press releases, cover letters, attention grabbing mail outs, new product promotional rollouts, classified ads, space ads, faxes, scripts, web pages to email marketing – anything where you need to communicate with clients can be enhanced with the right words.

Call Troy today at 403.259.4566 or fax 403.259.2092. Be sure and ask for your 3 Ways To Grow Your Business Report. Thank you for joining the other Entrepreneurial Spirits across the world and wish you the best in your quest for success.

You can write to:
Fresh Idea Company
183 Flavelle Rd SE, Calgary, Alberta, Canada T2H1G1

Websites:

www.smallbusinesscopywriter.com
www.calgaryadclinic.com
www.marketingesp.com
www.entrepreneurialspirits.com

What Makes Troy's Writing Ability Any Different Than Other Writers? Accountability – and results. 99% of writers are not trained properly on creating sales and marketing campaigns that produce substantial, measurable profits. Imagine knowing exactly how much profit is generated from every single marketing dollar spent. When it's working – you know it and can keep doing it. When it isn't working, stop doing it and move on...

GIVE THE GIFT OF THIS EXTRAORDINARY BOOK TO FAMILY, FRIENDS AND COLLEAGUES…

Yes, I want ________ copies of **Entrepreneurial Spirits** for $47.00 US each, plus $5 shipping.

Plus add the following to my order:

1) Profit Secrets Revealed – The Primer For Small Business - $17

2) Marketing ESP – 3 Steps To Miraculous Marketing Success
Home study course and audios - $127

My check or money order for $_________is enclosed.

Please charge my:

O Mastercard   O Visa   O American Express

Name:____

Company Name:________________________________

Address (incl. Postal code): ________________________

____

Ph:( )______________________**Fax:**( )______________

E-Mail: ______________________________________

Name on Credit Card:___________________________

Number:____________________________**Exp:**__________

Signature:____

Please mail with payment to:

Fresh Idea Company
183 Flavelle Rd SE
Calgary, Alberta
Canada T2H-1G1

Or:

Call your credit order in to 1.877.259.4566
Or fax to 1.403.259.2092
Email: troy@entrepreneurialspirits.com

Please note – credit card orders will be processed through Fresh Idea Company. Please note this for your statement. Thank you.

To your Entrepreneurial Spirit!

Troy White